I0458904

Resilient Hearts

Shaping Perspective, Embracing the Reframe

Josh Langer

Dedication

To Marsha, Samuel, Julia, and Vivian... this book was born with each of you in mind and written first for your hearts.

Acknowledgment

This book took shape in the furnace of hard seasons, though its spark has burned in me for years. One thing is certain: Without Jesus, there would be no story to tell.

Marsha, thank you for your steady encouragement and for giving me space to pour into this project.

Mama and Papa, twenty-four years ago I left Germany, and you released me—hesitantly at first—into the calling I sensed from God. Thank you! Now, as a parent myself, I feel the cost of that gift. *Danke, Mama und Papa! Ich hab euch lieb.*

And thank you to Bob Collins at KDP Publishing, your patience and expertise turned a rookie author into a published one. Thank you for guiding every step with care.

Your journey matters. Thank you for letting mine walk alongside yours. Tag me **@JoshTLanger** so I can cheer you on in your resilient adventures…

Endorsement

"I met Josh about 20 years ago and have watched him grow as both a worshiper and a leader. His love for God and people is undeniable, which is why I was able to wholeheartedly pass on the role of worship pastor to him at the church I led for many years. Josh is a great man with a deep well of wisdom, and I know he has a lot of good things to say."

Paul Baloche—American Christian Music Artist, Worship Leader, and Singer-songwriter

"Josh Langer lays his pain and trials bare on the pages of this book for all to see. With raw honesty, he shares the doubt, despair, and deep wrestling he has walked through. For anyone who has felt their world crumbling around them, Josh offers a voice of authentic vulnerability—speaking to the dark night of the soul while pointing to hope, forgiveness, and healing."

Steve Roquemore—Development Director at Mentoring Alliance

"I'm excited about this book! Josh is a gifted encourager, communicator, and leader who passionately champions others— especially young people—by calling out their gifts and helping them step out in faith. His love for Marsha and his kids is evident, and his genuine care for those around him leaves a lasting impact."

Debbie Lascelles—Love Mercy International

"Josh embodies honesty, integrity, and a deep commitment to truth. I've always trusted his sincerity and admired his unwavering care for people. His heart for others and pastoral spirit are truly evident in all he does."

Brad Stanley—USA Urban Missions Leadership Circle and author of books, "Finding God in the City" and "Unwilling To Concede"

Table of Contents

Introduction:
It's Not About Guarantees, But About Grace[1]

What if the hardest year of your life could become one of the most important chapters of your story? This book is about resilience—not the kind that fits neatly onto an inspirational poster, but the kind forged in the middle of chaos, questions, and pain. The kind that demands a change in one's perspective.

This book is born out of an enormously difficult time for me and my family. One thing after another seemed to unravel, and just when we thought we'd caught our breath, something else would hit. In the middle of it all, someone told me, "You should write down and share your thoughts." At first, I chuckled. What did I have to offer? I didn't have it all figured out, and honestly, I was just trying to survive most days. But the more I thought about it, the more I realized that I learned more in those many moments of struggle than I had in years of smooth sailing. And that kind of learning might just be worth sharing.

---

[1] **Grace:** God's love, forgiveness, and kindness, given freely even though we don't deserve it.

1

Hard times are exactly that—hard. My family and I walked through many seasons of pain and loss. I can't sugarcoat it: those days were messy and deeply heart-wrenching. We faced countless tears, sleepless nights, and aching questions that seemed to echo endlessly. But, strangely, we discovered something invaluable in the middle of all that brokenness. Brokenness, it turns out, is often the prerequisite[2] for growth and resilience.

I was broken, and in that brokenness, I began to see what I had been blind to for so long—my pride, shortcomings, and unhealthy securities. I learned the danger of bitterness and how it tries to steal what little strength you have left. I saw how much I depended on things that held no growth or value for me. When God began dismantling those structures, it hurt. I wanted to throw a tantrum and cling desperately to what I believed I deserved. Why would You take this from me? Don't I deserve better? I've served You for so many years, and this is what I get?

It all boiled down to one ugly truth: I thought I'd make a better god than Him.

How prideful am I? How tightly do I cling to my plans, ways, stuff, and version of security? I didn't want to let go. I didn't want to trust God—or anyone else for that matter—because what if they

---

[2] **Prerequisite:** Something that must happen first before something else can happen.

failed me? Beneath all my anger was fear. I was scared, unstable, and in desperate need of a reframe. And in that raw, unfiltered state, I realized how much I needed Jesus. Not the polished, Sunday-morning religious version, but the real God of the universe. The breaking hurts, but it reveals what needs to be healed. The tearing down makes room for God to rebuild.

Initially, I wrote this book for my kids. I wanted them to have something they could turn to when life gets messy. In fact, they might still be my only audience—and that's okay. But if you're holding this book in your hands, I know you'll greatly benefit from it, too. Not because I've arrived at some ultimate understanding of life's mysteries but because I've walked through enough storms to slowly realize that resilience isn't just about bouncing back. It's about the transformation that can occur, the beauty even amid the ashes. It's about finding God in the chaos and learning to trust Him even when nothing makes sense. It isn't about guarantees but about grace. So, if you're looking for something polished and perfect, this probably isn't the book for you. But if you're willing to dive into the mess, wrestle with some hard questions, and maybe even laugh a little along the way—keep reading. You're in good company.

Perspective Matters

In times when resilience is needed, our perspective and how we look at things matters most. Perspective and our focus allow us to zero in on what truly matters, filtering out the noise of fear, frustration, and distraction. It's the discipline to keep our eyes fixed on the next right step rather than getting overwhelmed by the entirety of the mountain ahead. Perspective is the lens through which we interpret our challenges. It transforms obstacles into opportunities and setbacks into stepping stones. Perspective doesn't just ground us in the present task; it also lifts our gaze to the bigger picture, reminding us that every trial has a purpose, and every detour is a lesson.

Over the years in pastoral ministry and my cross-cultural adventures in world missions, one undeniable truth has emerged: perspective is everything. Yes, everything; how you view the world, your circumstances, and even your heart profoundly shapes how you navigate life. Perspective isn't just a lens—it's the whole camera. Especially in tumultuous times, when life feels like a chaotic storm, your viewpoint can be the anchor that keeps you grounded or the gale force that sweeps you off course.

I've come to realize that perspective is more than just a concept; it's a skill, a discipline, and often even the lifeline that can lead to a resilient heart. That's why I've structured this book around the word "PERSPECTIVE," using it as an acrostic mnemonic[3] to

---

[3] **Acrostic Mnemonic:** A memory trick where each letter in a word stands for something else. (Like P-E-R-S-P-E-C-T-I-V-E)

name the chapters. I want these ideas to stick. True perspective is transformative. It allows us to see beyond our circumstances, embrace the lessons hidden in hardships, and find resilience when life feels unmanageable.

As difficult as it is in times of chaos, expanding our perspective often induces emotional level-headedness. It allows us to see beyond the immediate moment at the bigger picture. When we focus solely on the present crisis, our emotions can feel overwhelming, but when we step back and view our circumstances in light of eternity, peace often follows. The apostle Paul models this mindset in 2 Corinthians 4:17-18, where he writes,

"For our light and momentary troubles are achieving for us an eternal glory that far outweighs them all. So we fix our eyes not on what is seen, but on what is unseen."

Paul's ability to resiliently endure suffering came from his perspective shift—recognizing that temporary challenges were shaping something far greater. Trusting that God's purposes extend beyond our understanding cultivates emotional balance. So, as you journey through this book, let each chapter be a reminder that perspective is not only something you can gain—it is something you must cultivate.

Before we dive any further into this book, I need to add a quick disclaimer. As I write about perspective and resilience, I'm fully aware that we are all shaped by our experiences, worldview, communities, and backgrounds. I am not here to compare one trauma with another, but I also know that there are people in this world enduring unimaginable suffering. Many people are facing abuse, deep depression, loss, war, fear, and night after night, real monsters. Evil is real, and it would be immensely naive to think that a few principles of resilience alone could erase it. Yet, I do believe we all have a responsibility to build resilience because, without it, we'd be powerless to do anything in the face of such darkness.

I want to grow in my trust in a good God who will ultimately redeem the cosmos, make all things new, and bring justice for both the victim and the perpetrator. Everything that is out of order will come back into order because God promised it. John Eldredge writes: "No more tears. No more pain. No more death. No longer any reason to mourn. At the renewal of all things, our hearts are going to be free from grief."[4] We must not let the weight of the world's evil or our own struggles paralyze us. Instead, we are called to pursue resilience, strengthening ourselves in the Lord to give, build, love, and be part of the change this world desperately needs. God invites us to partner with Him, to create with Him, to bring Heaven to Earth with Him, and to find resilience in the face

---

[4] Eldredge, J. (2017). *All Things New: Heaven, Earth, and the Restoration of Everything You Love.* Thomas Nelson.

of evil because He is with us. In this divine partnership, our efforts are not just acts of survival but acts of sacred purpose, reflecting God's glory and advancing His Kingdom.

This book is about finding clarity in chaos, standing firm when the ground shakes, and holding onto hope when the world feels dim. Every chapter of this book explores how what we choose to focus on shapes our ability to grow resilient. Resilience isn't something that just happens; it's cultivated through deliberate attention to the right things. Whether it's anchoring ourselves in timeless truths, learning to see adversity as opportunity, or finding strength in relationships, our focus determines how we rise—or fall—in the face of challenges. This book will guide you through practical and profound ways to adjust your perspective, set your sights on what truly matters, and build the inner fortitude to weather life's storms. Resilience isn't built in comfort—it's forged in the fire. And in that fire, focus sharpens, revealing the path that truly leads forward.

Chapter 1
P – Pivot[5] in Chaos

As 2024 unfolded with its chaos, confusion, and exhaustion, I found myself asking a hard but essential question: Is Jesus really enough for me? When life stripped away the roles, the applause, and the sense of purpose I had wrapped my identity in, I realized how much I had anchored my worth to things that could—and did—vanish. The accolades, the recognition, the sense of achievement—all gone in an instant, leaving a hollow space where certainty once resided. Would Jesus still be enough when the applause faded into silence? Would He still be enough when the music stopped, and I felt the ache of purposelessness? Would He still be enough when I felt forgotten, longing for the approval and affirmation of others? These were not hypothetical questions but gut-level struggles. And yet, in the stillness of those moments, a deeper truth began to emerge: Jesus doesn't offer fleeting applause, flattery, or shallow affirmation; He offers Himself—steadfast,[6] unchanging, always present. The challenge wasn't whether He was enough but whether I was willing to let go of everything else to discover that He always has been.

---

[5] **Pivot:** To make a change in strategy, direction, or perspective.
[6] **Steadfast:** Often used in the Bible to describe God's unwavering nature.

Here is What Happened

June 4, 2024, will forever be etched into our family's history as a surreal, life-altering day. By midmorning, around 10:30am, our lives would be turned upside down. It began with an ominous creak, then a thunderous crash as the gigantic oak tree, which had stood in our backyard for decades, came tumbling down, its branches tearing through the roof and into the heart of our home.

My wife Marsha and our ten-year-old daughter, Julia, were in the kitchen that gloomy day, looking out the window as the towering oak tree began its descent toward our home. With the instincts only a mother possesses, Marsha grabbed Julia and sprinted to the other side of the house, their hearts pounding in sync with the Earth's tremors. The days leading up to this moment had been soaked in relentless rain, saturating the ground until it could no longer bear the weight of that ancient giant. The night before had been a different kind of storm. The power had gone out, leaving our home in darkness. Our city was struggling with the onslaught of weather-related calamities, and the rain seemed determined to wash away every semblance of normalcy. Little did we know, as we lay in bed, listening to the rain drum incessantly on the roof,that this would be the last night we would sleep in that room as it was. If that tree had chosen the night to fall, it would have been a catastrophe of unimaginable proportions. One of its mighty branches had crashed down precisely where Marsha and I slept. The darkness would have magnified the chaos and confusion, making the escape even more perilous. Thank you, Jesus, for your protection!

I was paralyzed in disbelief and fear as the sound reverberated through the walls. The initial shock rendered me motionless, unable to process the destruction unfolding around us. I never liked feeling helpless and powerless. Thankfully, our community rallied around us in ways that we could never have imagined. Friends, co-workers, neighbors, and even acquaintances we barely knew showed up, ready to help. They moved quickly, clearing out almost the entire house and making crucial decisions while I stood in a daze, my mind struggling to catch up with the chaos.

People react to crisis and calamity differently, and our family was no exception. Samuel (12), ever the practical one, went straight to securing his valued Legos, ensuring not a single brick was out of place or left behind. Meanwhile, Julia (10), with tears in her eyes, skipped the small talk and dove right into deep theological questions, pondering the meaning of it all. Vivian (7), on the other hand, was a bit unaware, across the yard in our barn with her friends playing, nearly missing the whole calamity altogether.

While I was paralyzed by the shock and the magnitude of the

disaster that day, Marsha pushed through with a determination I can only describe as heroic (perhaps with a hint of denial). She directed the chaos, guiding people through the house, grabbing what she could, and helping wherever possible. The next day, as the adrenaline wore off, she crumbled into tears, and I found the mental and physical strength to take the reins. In the days that followed, we traded off being the emotional pillar for each other. When one of us faltered, the other stood firm, demonstrating the ebb and flow of resilience and vulnerability that define true partnership and love. Genuine resilience requires genuine relationships. None of us is meant to do this alone. "Today, if we have no peace, it is because we have forgotten that we belong to each other – that man, that woman, that child is my brother or my sister. If everyone could see the image of God in his neighbor, do you think we would still need tanks and generals?"[7]

Two Strangers with Chainsaws in Our Bedroom

At one point, two strangers wielding chainsaws were in our bedroom, meticulously cutting away the branches that had pierced through our sanctuary. The sight was almost absurd—a stark contrast to the tranquil, safe haven our bedroom had always been.

---

[7] Mother Teresa (2010). *Where There Is Love, There Is God: A Path to Closer Union with God and Greater Love for Others*, p.330

It felt like a scene from a horror movie, a bizarre blend of the ordinary and the catastrophic. These men, with their relentless buzz of chainsaws, became unlikely heroes, helping us to take the first steps toward recovery.

As I walked through our gutted home in the following days, memories of the past 20 years flooded back. Every room held a story, a piece of our family's journey. The living room where we celebrated birthdays and Christmases, the kitchen where we shared countless meals and conversations, and the bedrooms where dreams were nurtured and fears were soothed. All now lay in ruins, reminding us of the fragility of the physical things we hold dear.

Amid the wreckage, many profound lessons began to emerge. Psalm 119:67 says,

"Before I was afflicted, I went astray, but now I keep Your word."

There are truths and strengths that we only discover through hardship. Family therapist Nicole Zasowki, in her book *What If It's Wonderful*, insightfully observes: "Life doesn't have to be hard to be holy."[8] I think that's really true. None of us need to chase after some form of asceticism.[9] Sure, the Bible teaches self-discipline and denying oneself for the sake of following Jesus (Luke 9:23, 1

---

[8] Zasowski, N. (2022). *What If It's Wonderful?: An Invitation to Release Your Fears, Choose Joy, and Find the Courage to Celebrate.* Thomas Nelson.
[9] **Asceticism:** Severe self-discipline and avoidance of indulgence.

Corinthians 9:27), but it does not endorse extreme self-inflicted suffering as a means to earn holiness or favor with God.

Nevertheless, resilience is often forged in the fires of adversity, and this experience was no different. We began to learn the art of leaning on each other and, more importantly, leaning on God. Difficult times often strip away the superficial layers of our lives, revealing what truly matters. In this trial, our family discovered that life can be really hard at times, but we also discovered a deeper reliance on God and on one another. It sure was a time of testing and unmatched growth.

Walking through the shell of our home, I felt a mix of sorrow and determination. This place, which had seen so much joy, yelling, hugs, tears, mistakes, and laughter, was now an embodiment of our resilience (or lack of it). We slowly, began to see that while the physical structure was damaged, the foundation of our family – our trust in God, love, and commitment to one another – remained foundational. It was as if God was telling us that while earthly things may falter, He remained our steadfast refuge.

The journey of rebuilding our home and our lives was neither quick nor easy. It pretty much felt like waiting for a sloth to finish a marathon. My patience reservoirs were depleted.[10] There were days of frustration, many moments of doubt, and nights of weariness. Yet, through it all, we experienced the power of community, the importance of patience (that was perhaps the hardest lesson for me to grasp), overcoming the paralyzing effects of helplessness, facing down reality while searching for meaning in it all, and the strength that comes from trusting that God has our back. Romans 5:3-4 says,

"Not only so, but we also glory in our sufferings, because we know that suffering produces perseverance; perseverance, character; and character, hope."

The Bible teaches us that God uses moments of crisis to refine us, to teach us, and to draw us closer to Him. While I firmly believe God did not cause the tree to fall, He certainly began to teach us through the experience. As James 1:2-4 reminds us,

"Consider it pure joy, my brothers and sisters, whenever you face trials of many kinds, because you know that the testing of your faith produces perseverance. Let perseverance finish its work so that you may be mature and complete, not lacking anything."

In all this mess lies something I need. Every trial contains a teaching, hidden treasures of wisdom. Within all this chaos and

---

[10] **Depletion:** A state of being drained or emptied of emotional, physical, or spiritual energy.

disruption lies something essential for our growth. Problems, as painful as they are, can cultivate perseverance, which molds us into maturity and completeness, leaving us lacking in nothing. What a profound and, yes, uncomfortable truth. But it is real, and it is unavoidable. Resilience doesn't come any other way.

But There Was More

This tree situation came at an interesting and pivotal time. The work and ministry we had poured our hearts into for 23 years had begun to crumble before our eyes. When self-assessment and evaluation are viewed as distractions from an organization's mission rather than essential tools for its health and growth, trouble inevitably follows. Neglecting intentional reflection[11] creates blind spots that fester—leading to burnout, confusion, and growing disillusionment at every level.

In such environments, leadership often defaults to top-down control rather than collaborative discernment, fostering an unhealthy hierarchy that stifles innovation and honest dialogue. Ideas are dismissed based on the age or status of the person who presents them rather than their merit, and frustration takes root when people feel unheard or unseen.

Over time, what was once a shared mission begins to unravel

---

[11] **Intentional reflection:** Purposefully thinking through and processing life experiences rather than avoiding or ignoring them.

under the weight of unaddressed tensions and unexamined practices. I've seen this firsthand—the slow erosion that eventually gives way to a complete organizational breakdown, not because the mission lacked importance but because the willingness to pause, reflect, and recalibrate was seen as weakness rather than wisdom.

Marsha, I, and many others had fought hard for much-needed changes on our campus, pressing on tirelessly against a relentless tide of outdated patterns and resistance. But despite our efforts, things didn't change, and we watched helplessly as many dear friends left along the way. Financial strain, coupled with a deep unwillingness at every level of leadership to face necessary change, threatened the very heart of our ministry. I wrestled with other leaders for what felt like an eternity, engaging in conversation after conversation that went nowhere until finally, we reached the point where we realized we were in the middle of what Henry Cloud calls a "necessary ending."[12]

My tendency to hold on to things for too long, perhaps out of stubborn hope or sheer tenacity, was put to the test once more. Our home, where we had lived and loved, and our spiritual mission, where we had invested our entire adult lives until now, both fell apart in tandem. 2024 was a year that tested our faith, resilience,

---

[12] Cloud, D. H., PhD. (2010). *Necessary Endings - The Employees, Businesses, And Relationships That All Of Us Have To Give Up In Order To Move Forward.* HarperCollins Publishers Inc.

and commitment to each other and our calling. As we navigated the rubble of our home and the disarray of our ministry, we were forced to confront the depths of our endurance and trust in God's character and promises. This dual crisis shook us to our core. Yet, it also offered an unparalleled opportunity for growth, reflection, readjustment, and, ultimately, a deeper reliance on Jesus. Henry Cloud says it bluntly: "Being alive requires that we sometimes kill off things in which we were once invested, uproot what we previously nurtured, and tear down what we built for an earlier time."[13]

This ordeal taught us that true resilience is not about never falling but trusting God's character, even when the path is unclear. Some of those lessons are tough, really tough. We need to be honest about our struggles. We need to feel the pain and learn to grieve. We will bend under the weight of our burdens, but we don't need to break. We can be shaken but not shattered, perplexed but never plunged into despair. Resilience isn't about being flawless or untouchable; it's about acknowledging our imperfections and finding the strength to keep moving forward despite the heartache.

As a family, we began to understand that resilience is cultivated through trials. It is in these moments of suffering that our faith is deepened and our own character is refined. Looking

---

[13] Cloud, D. H., Phd. (2010). *Necessary Endings* - HarperCollins Publishers Inc.

back, we can truly see God's hand in every step. He provided for us through the kindness of others, gave us the strength to endure, and used this experience to teach us invaluable lessons. We learned to trust Him more, to lean on each other, and to appreciate the blessings we often take for granted.

And, There Was Even More

2024 had even more twists and turns than we anticipated. After saving for two years, we had planned a long-awaited family trip to Germany to celebrate my dad's 80th birthday—a milestone we couldn't wait to honor. But then, life threw us a curveball: the tree that fell on our house left us questioning if we should cancel the trip altogether. We hesitated, but wise voices encouraged us, saying, "The house will still be there when you get back, but your dad only turns 80 once. You must go!" And so, with mixed emotions, we went. It turned out to be a deeply meaningful journey—filled with moments of reconnecting with my roots, savoring the beauty of Germany, and enjoying precious time with family over delicious meals. But the emotions ran deep, knowing how fragile everything felt. Just a few months later, my mom fell in the bathtub and broke her leg, and my dad, already struggling with his health, lost consciousness unexpectedly. Their health challenges escalated, and not being able to be there for them as much as I wanted was heartbreaking. With everything else going on, I found myself dreaming almost nightly about these struggles as if my mind couldn't let go, still trying to solve problems while I slept. I kept asking myself, 'How can I heal if I'm still fighting?' It was a time of relentless stress, anxiety, questions, and hardship—a season I wouldn't wish on anyone, yet one that taught me more than I ever expected.

Why Some People Thrive Under Pressure

Have you ever wondered why some people seem to thrive under pressure while others crumble? What does it mean to hold onto faith when life feels like it's falling apart? How do we reconcile Jesus' promise of an abundant life with the reality of pain, suffering, and unmet expectations? Is it possible to be resilient in a world where everything feels uncertain? What if the key lies in something—or someone—unchanging? How do you keep your faith alive when the weight of life seems unbearable? What if the life you're building isn't about avoiding suffering but learning how to suffer well? Could resilience and faith grow stronger in the fire? What if resilience isn't about bouncing back but about moving forward differently—transformed, not just restored? Can you detect the pivot here?

In one of his letters to a struggling Navy SEAL friend, Eric Greitens writes: "Pain can break us or make us wiser. Suffering can destroy us or make us stronger. Fear can cripple, or it can make us more courageous. It is resilience that makes the difference... resilience is a virtue as old as human existence."

Greitens continues: "Human beings can turn hardship into wisdom because we are born with the capacity for resilience, and we can make ourselves more resilient through practice. To be resilient—to build a full and meaningful life of strength, wisdom, and joy—is not easy. But it's not complicated. We can all do it. To get there, it's not enough to want to be resilient or to think about being resilient. We have to choose to live a resilient life."[14]

Resilience isn't about simply bouncing back quickly or slapping a success story on top of the pain. Sometimes, an enormous amount of patience is needed in the pursuit of resilience. We often learn the most when we're at our weakest, most defenseless, and we don't have to rush through those moments just to have a neat testimony; we need to learn to pivot in them. Have you noticed that often, it's in suffering that we learn the most and perhaps the fastest? Tragedy and trauma have a way of getting our attention like nothing else. They force us to reconsider what's truly important and cause us to listen to the quiet, painful truths we often ignore.

This season of uprooting in our early 40s was such a time for

---

[14] Greitens, E. (2015). *Resilience: Hard-won Wisdom for Living a Better Life.* Houghton Mifflin Harcourt.

my wife and me. It was a time of deep soul-searching, of letting go of old patterns of thinking, and of being willing to adjust our perspective and course in ways we had resisted for too long or didn't even know needed adjusting. During that time, every assumption, every habit, every way of thinking was challenged and reexamined. Every change felt significant, a step toward a better, more intentional way of living. Resilience doesn't mean denying the pain or pretending everything is fine—it means working through it, letting it shape us, and rising stronger and different.

As I reflected on 2024—with all its pain, mystery, stress, and challenges—I came face-to-face with a simple but profound truth: life is messy, unpredictable, and often an uphill battle. Yet, in the midst of the chaos, I realized that one of the greatest gifts is the courage and wisdom to keep moving forward. Not perfectly, not always gracefully, but steadily, step by step, learning to navigate the hard places with resilience and trust in God.

I've always said to my kids, "Don't just settle for your best, but look for ways to get better." Resilience is all about asking the hard questions, regularly checking in with yourself, and being open to a pivot and a perspective change. It's about keeping a soft heart and staying open to what God is saying and what is truly happening in and around you. Today, instead of hardening your heart, listen to Jesus. Part of resilience is being able to take feedback, even criticism, without getting defensive. It's about looking in the mirror and being okay that we are all still a work in progress. It means getting honest about the patterns in our lives that are holding us back—no matter how comfortable or convenient they might feel. Resistance to change is the enemy of resilience; the more we fight it, the harder it is to grow.

In *We Who Wrestled With God*, Jordan Peterson observes, "Life is well portrayed as a series of uphill journeys. For pessimists, that is the fate of Sisyphus, doomed to roll a rock up a mountain … only to have it roll back down. A more optimistic interpreter might see instead the opportunities for personal transformation. When we have climbed a new mountain … we have brought something successfully to an end … and become more than we were."[15]

This perspective aligns beautifully with the way God shapes us through life's challenges. He's not merely interested in us recovering from hardship; He's molding us into something greater through it.

Let the Song Settle in Your Heart

In the shifting, stay rooted. I remember when I used to drop off my kids at kindergarten. As we walked up to the door, I would

---

[15] Peterson, J. B. (2024). *We Who Wrestle with God: Perceptions of the Divine.* Random House.

start singing a simple chorus, and they'd join in: "This is the day, this is the day that the Lord has made. Let us rejoice and be glad in it!" It was my way of giving them a tune to carry in their hearts, a melody that could brighten their day when it got tough.

One Saturday afternoon, as they played together in the living room, I heard that same chorus ring out, sung by my kids all on their own. It caught me off guard and filled me with joy to realize the song had become part of them, already taking root in their hearts. This book is about that same kind of melody—a chorus of hope and trust in God's goodness that can carry us through even the roughest days.

Even though I have been a worship pastor for many years, don't worry, this isn't a book on church worship; it's more about finding the grit to sing in any storm, the courage to dance in the rain, the peace to pivot to gain a new perspective, and the vision to see triumph woven into trouble. It's about discovering a chorus in the heart of chaos and realizing there's a song that never leaves us, even when life hits a sour note. In short, this is a book on the journey of resilience—but probably not in the way you'd expect. Again, it's not just about bouncing back; it's about learning to hear harmony even in dissonance and growing stronger with each note, high and low.

Since hardship, loss, and suffering are unavoidable in life, learning resilience is perhaps one of the most valuable lessons we can learn and pass on. Hence, this book! Life is filled with unexpected challenges—moments when the ground feels like it has been swept from under our feet. As a father, I find it crucial to prepare my children not only to face these storms but to sing during them and eventually to rise above them. It's about teaching our kids that pain and difficulty are not the end of the story but the beginning of a new chapter of growth and transformation.

By sharing our own experiences of hardship and how we navigated them with faith, tears, confidence, failure, determination, and even humor, we can impart a powerful message. Resilience isn't merely about enduring hardship; it's about emerging from it stronger, changed for the better, with a greater capacity to contend with life's complexities and pursue meaning. It's about trusting God's promise that He suffers alongside us and that He is with us in the fire, refining us as gold. It's about instilling in my kids the belief that they have the inner strength through the Holy Spirit to walk through the valley of the shadow of death when necessary. These lessons aren't just for children but for all of us. These lessons, forged in the crucible of life's trials, will equip us to face our own futures with courage, hope, and childlike trust in good God.

Off its Axis

A pastor friend once prayed: "Lord, in life, we often tend to switch on autopilot.[16] Thank you, that sometimes life throws us off balance so drifting along numbly is not an option."

There are certain things we will never truly learn unless we are thrown off balance from time to time and almost forced to pivot. When life seems off its axis, tragedy strikes, and the weight of suffering feels unbearable, we can remember that these are the moments that shape us. They teach us resilience, deepen our faith, and remind us that with God as our anchor, we are enabled to weather the storm and sing in it.

I sat across from a friend, both of us reeling from the fallout of the unjust chaos that had upended the ministry we'd poured decades of our lives into. As we talked, we processed our anger, confusion, and heartbreak. We prayed together, and then, out of nowhere, he said, "Thank you, Lord, for your gift of disruption." I thought he was joking—some sort of gallows humor to lighten the heaviness of our prayer. But he wasn't. He kept going, thanking God for the chaos, the uprooting, and the fact that nothing was normal anymore. He prayed, "Lord, if everything were normal— normal habits, normal schedules—we'd never be in a position of

---

[16] **Autopilot living:** Going through life without conscious awareness or intention.

deep self-evaluation or soul searching."

I sat there stunned, letting his words sink in. He was absolutely right. Disruption, as much as it shakes us and strips us of comfort, forces us to pause, reevaluate, and confront the areas of life we've left unchecked. When life is predictable, it's easy to fall into the trap of thinking we're in control. But disruption? It pulls the rug out from under us and compels us to face truths we'd rather avoid. It's uncomfortable, yes, but also deeply transformative. As he finished his prayer, I realized how often I'd cursed disruption rather than welcomed it as the uninvited but necessary teacher it can be. Sometimes, the chaos births clarity, the uprooting that makes way for growth.

To see what you need to see, you must pivot your vision and fix your attention where it counts—because clarity demands a shift. In this world, so many things are clamoring for our attention, some alluring and others troubling. Yet, the true challenge lies in maintaining a steady focus on what truly matters, even when chaos strikes. For every moment, every experience, every failure, every joy, and every trial are opportunities to practice this focus. Just as an athlete hones their skills through repetition, we too can cultivate this skill.

Growing in that skill as a parent is like training for an Olympic sport you never signed up for—but with higher stakes and way more Lego injuries. Kids have an uncanny knack for interrupting your oh-so-precious rhythms, those sacred routines you cherish. They don't just ask questions; they bombard you with them. My son, for example, can give TED Talks on his latest Lego creations, complete with in-depth architectural details. While I admire his genius, sometimes I just want a moment of silence. But here's the kicker: marriage and parenting are designed to dethrone you. You can either grumble about your disrupted kingdom or embrace the fact that the throne was never yours to begin with.

I've read more self-help books than I care to admit, all promising to reveal the secrets to a better life. The advice is always the same: "All you need is a plan and a little commitment."

Sure, that sounds great until you realize most of these books were probably written by single people with no kids. I used to pride myself on having my ducks neatly in a row. Then my kids came along, and let me tell you, they didn't just scatter the ducks; they staged a full-blown duckpocalypse. Feathers everywhere. No survivors. Turns out, parenting isn't about getting your ducks in a row—it's about learning to love (or at least survive) the chaos of the whole flock going rogue. Kids take an eternity to order at restaurants, siblings bicker like it's their full-time job, and irrational behavior is basically a rite of passage. You can fight it— get frustrated every time your plans are upended and everything feels off its axis—or you can recognize these moments as divine opportunities to flex your resilience muscle.

Have you noticed that life generally doesn't cater to your preferences? The art we can all learn is to stay focused—or regain our perspective—during turmoil when we feel off balance, and it often requires pivoting. True resilience grows when you surrender your rights, pivot, change your focus, and allow your preferences to be altered. So, I need to learn to listen to my son describe his A-frame Lego house for the 100th time and engage with my daughters' endless, yet truly delightful, questions. My family and I had to relearn the rhythms of daily life when the tree crashed into our home, and our workplace crumbled around us.

In *Good Catastrophe*, Benjamin Windle challenges the prevailing narrative that happiness is only found in a problem-free life. He writes, "What if we could fundamentally reframe how we see life's challenges? The story that the 'good life'—the life of happiness, success, and health—is somehow predicated on us eliminating problems, adversity, and challenges is not working... we have to get good at handling the bad."[17]

Windle's insight is profound because it shifts the focus from avoidance to mastery. True resilience, as he suggests, isn't about

---

[17] Windle, B. (2023). *Good Catastrophe: The Tide-Turning Power of Hope.* Baker Books.

living without hardship but about learning to navigate it with strength and purpose. This reframing feels radical and deeply necessary in a world obsessed with comfort and convenience. Life's challenges aren't interruptions to our happiness but invitations to grow, stretch, pivot, and find meaning. The real "good life" begins when we stop running from adversity and start leaning into it with courage.

One of the hardest lessons I've learned is that resilience isn't primarily about results at all—it's about who we become in the process. We live in a culture obsessed with outcomes, where success is measured by trophies, titles, and tangible milestones. Because of this, I never enjoyed feeling off balance, and I often found myself blaming the process when things didn't turn out the way I expected, as though the difficulty of the journey was somehow the problem. But the truth is, resilience is forged in the process, not in the results. It's in the long, unseen hours of effort, failure, and perseverance that true strength is born. Yet, we resist this because we're so result-oriented, so addicted to quick wins, that we try to sidestep the pain of the process entirely. But avoiding the process is like skipping training for a marathon and expecting to cross the finish line strong. Growth doesn't happen in the moment of achievement; it happens in the grind, the setbacks, and the daily decisions to keep going. Resilience isn't about avoiding pain; it's about embracing it as a teacher and letting it shape us. Results may come and go, but the person we become in the process is what truly matters.

Pivoting in the Pain

Pain is inevitable. Whether it comes from shattered dreams, failed plans, or losses that leave us breathless, pain shows up uninvited. The real question is: what do we do when life doesn't go as planned? How do we alter our course when the path we carefully charted crumbles beneath our feet? How do we remain alive when everything around us feels like it's dying? These questions aren't just theoretical—they're existential. To pivot in the pain is to adapt, to grow, and to move forward not just as survivors but as transformed individuals.

Pain often feels like the absence of God. The Book of Job is a profound exploration of human suffering, divine sovereignty, false conceptions of who God is, and trust in the midst of uncertainty. It opens with Job, a righteous man blessed with wealth, health, and a large family. Unbeknownst to Job, a heavenly conversation takes place in which accusers challenge God, arguing that Job's faithfulness is dependent on His blessings. God permits the accusers to test Job by stripping him of his possessions, family, and health, but not his life.

In his suffering, Job wrestles with profound questions about God's justice and the nature of human suffering yet remains sinless. His friends, Eliphaz, Bildad, and Zophar, arrive to comfort him but instead accuse him of wrongdoing, insisting that his suffering must be a punishment for sin. Job refutes their arguments, maintaining his innocence while lamenting his plight and questioning why the righteous suffer.

In the climactic chapters, we see that God doesn't very often answer questions directly but unfolds stories. God reveals His power and wisdom through a series of rhetorical questions about the universe's complexity. This response humbles Job, leading him to acknowledge God's goodness and sovereignty and his own limited understanding. In the end, God restores Job's fortunes, doubling what he had before, and rebukes his friends for their misguided counsel.

Summarizing the Book of Job in a few paragraphs almost feels like an injustice, as if reducing a masterpiece to a mere sketch. Job's story is raw and unfiltered—a journey through anguish, bewilderment, and, eventually, profound revelation. Admittedly, as you read, it can feel like a never-ending, frustrating dialogue between Job and his so-called friends. What are they even talking about? Their endless cycles of advice, blame, and defense can feel tedious, almost maddening. Job's struggle might seem overblown or tiresome for those who've never truly wrestled with deep suffering or loss.

Yet, for anyone who's been crushed under the weight of life's hardest blows, it's a mirror, reflecting the chaos of pain, our incessant desire for control, and the need for patience—not only with others but with ourselves. The book of Job teaches us that grief is not a sprint or a short film; it's an ongoing saga, often messy and unpredictable. It invites us to sit in the dust alongside those who mourn without rushing to fix them or explain their pain away. It reminds us that true compassion isn't tidy, and healing doesn't necessarily follow a script. It reminds us that God cannot be reduced to a means to an end or manipulated to serve our desires. If we're not careful, we can fall into the same flawed mindset as Job's friends, believing that living righteously earns us leverage with God to secure blessings or avoid hardship. Life is rarely as simple as the transactional equation we often wish it to be: "I do good, so I get good; I do bad, so I get bad." That's not how it works, is it? Life is far more complex, unpredictable, and full of mystery. Instead of trying to decode every outcome or control our circumstances, we are called to hold tightly to the unwavering goodness of God.

In Job's cries and questions, we find permission to wrestle with our own, and in God's eventual response, we glimpse a hope that's greater than our understanding. In Job 9:11, Job laments,

"If He passes by me, I would not see Him; if He moves past, I

would not perceive Him."

This verse encapsulates Job's struggle to sense God's presence amid his suffering. It serves as a poignant reminder for us today.

The Hebrew term for "pass by" (עָבַר, avar[18]) conveys motion or crossing over, suggesting God's transcendence[19] and the mysterious nature of His workings. Job acknowledges that God's presence, though real, can feel imperceptible in times of distress. This speaks to a universal human experience—feeling distant from God when life feels chaotic.

The phrase "I would not see Him" uses the Hebrew word רָאָה (ra'ah[20]), which implies perception or understanding. Here, Job recognizes the limits of human perspective, particularly in spiritual matters. In crises, our natural focus often narrows to immediate problems, blinding us to God's activity and care. Similarly, "were He to move" (חָלַף, chalaph[21]) reflects the dynamic and purposeful nature of God's actions, which often elude human comprehension because of our pride and unwillingness to pivot.

However, the Bible consistently calls us to walk in an ever-

---

[18] **Avar:** Means to cross or move over. Used in Job to express the mysterious, often unseen movement of God in our lives.

[19] **Transcendence:** The stunning reality that the God reigns above all creation.

[20] **Ra'ah:** Means to perceive or see. Job expresses the feeling of being unable to perceive God's presence, especially during suffering.

[21] **Chalaph:** Means to pass or change. This highlights the elusive, hard-to-understand nature of God's work from a human perspective.

increasing knowledge of God and His ways. One of my favorite Psalms is Psalm 25:14, as it reminds us,

"The secret of the Lord is with those who fear Him, and He will show them His covenant."

Even though crisis can obscure our vision of God, we need to remember that He is moving and actively working to build His Church and bring His kingdom to Earth. God desires to reveal His thoughts, intentions, and heart to us, inviting us to walk closely with Him.

In moments of crisis, this verse challenges us to rest in God and allow Him to recalibrate our perspective. The Bible is full of stories of people whose lives were derailed—Joseph betrayed by his brothers and sold into slavery, Job losing everything, Paul thrown into prison. Yet, in each instance, their suffering didn't diminish God's presence, purpose, and care. In fact, these detours became the very ground where God's purposes unfolded. Pivoting in the pain starts with the understanding that God is active and present in what appears to be a detour, working through the mess. He is not caught off guard by our setbacks. Instead, He calls us to trust Him when we can't see the road ahead, knowing that He can redeem even our deepest losses.

Viktor Frankl, a Holocaust survivor, wrote about pivoting in chaos and finding meaning in suffering. He argued that when embraced rather than resisted, pain can propel us toward a deeper understanding of life and purpose. In *Man's Search for Meaning,* Viktor E. Frankl[22] paints a harrowing picture of life in a concentration camp, describing it as utterly hopeless.

One day, while toiling under the command of a particularly sadistic foreman, he became overwhelmed by how meaningless and trivial his life seemed. In that moment, he realized something crucial: to survive, he needed to pivot and find a purpose in the midst of pain. So, Frankl began to focus and to imagine himself after the war, giving lectures on the psychology of concentration camps and helping others understand the unimaginable horrors he endured. Even though he wasn't sure he'd make it out alive, he set this concrete goal for himself. In doing so, he transcended the suffering of the present moment and found a sense of meaning in the face of despair.

Naturally, my trauma pales in comparison to the unimaginable horrors of surviving a World War II concentration camp. However, writing this book became one of the ways of pivoting my focus amidst the struggle, turning pain into purpose and chaos into some clarity. Despite the loss, trauma, and hardship, the hope that my kids will one day read these words gives all the pain a sense of

---

[22] Frankl, V. E. (2013). *Man's Search For Meaning: The classic tribute to hope from the Holocaust.* Random House.

direction. It helps me rise above the difficulties, knowing that maybe, just maybe, this could serve them (and now you, too) in their own lives. There's power in purpose—whether you're trapped in unimaginable suffering or just trying to make sense of everyday struggles. When seen through the lens of purpose, pain becomes more than just suffering—it becomes a mentor.

8 Practical Steps to Pivot Well and Gain Resilience

1. Pause And Acknowledge.

It's okay to grieve. It's not just okay; it is necessary. Take time, really take time, to process what you've lost. Pain denied is pain multiplied. There is no recovery without recognition. Recognize your emotions, journal your thoughts, or talk to someone you trust. Naming the pain is the first step to overcoming it and recharging our soul.

One of my favorite articles on resilience is called *"Resilience Is About How You Recharge, Not How You Endure"* by Shawn Achor and Michelle Gielan.[23] I mean, the title alone is gold. It completely flips the script on what we often think resilience is about. They argue—and brilliantly so—that resilience isn't about

---

[23] Review, H. B., Goleman, D., Achor, S., & Sonnenfeld, J. A. (2017). *Resilience* (HBR Emotional Intelligence Series). Harvard Business School Press.

gritting your teeth and muscling through endless stress and pain like some kind of overworked superhero. No, real resilience, the kind that lasts, is about how well you recharge. It's about knowing when to step away, refuel, and give yourself permission to rest. One of the key points they make is that stopping does not equal recovering. Just because you're no longer working doesn't mean you're recharging. How many of us "stop" by scrolling through our phones, binging shows, or stressing about tomorrow? That's not recharging; that's just distracting. Recovery means creating intentional space-time to breathe, connect with God, do something life-giving, or even just sleep. It's about replenishing your emotional and physical energy, not just hitting pause while your stress simmers in the background. God literally built rest into the week with the Sabbath,[24] knowing we'd try to work ourselves into the ground otherwise. It's a reminder that resilience isn't just about hustle; it's about trust. Trusting that stepping back doesn't mean failure and that God designed us to thrive in a rhythm of work and rest. So, take a breath. Acknowledge your grief and pain. Recharge. Resilience isn't how long you can last—it's how well you reset. True recovery isn't accidental; it's intentional.

Henry Cloud describes the process of "metabolizing experiences" in his book *Necessary Endings*, saying, "In love and

---

[24] **Sabbath:** God's invitation to rest in His presence.

in work, experience is the 'food' of life. Just as 'you are what you eat,' you are what you experience as a person. You 'ingest' experience like food, taking it in, and it becomes part of you. To metabolize experience, whether in significant relationships or in business, you have to do what your body does with food: keep what is usable to you and eliminate what is not."[25]

This concept is vital when life throws us into chaos. Pivoting in the midst of turmoil requires more than just quick reactions—it demands intentional reflection. We cannot adjust our methods or embrace change without first pausing to acknowledge the weight of our grief and the reality of our emotions. Emotional intelligence[26] is the key here, enabling us to evaluate what's happening within and around us. Only by metabolizing our experiences, processing the pain, learning the lessons, and letting go of the unnecessary can we pivot effectively, transforming even the hardest seasons into opportunities for growth and resilience.

2. Try Fasting.

I'll start this off by saying that I am not an authority on this at all. Fasting is one of those spiritual disciplines that I approach with

---

[25] Cloud, H. (2011). *Necessary Endings: The Employees, Businesses, and Relationships That All of Us Have to Give Up in Order to Move Forward.* Zondervan.
[26] **Emotional intelligence:** The ability to be aware of, control, and express one's emotions.

both reluctance and reverence. Let me be honest—I'm not naturally drawn to it. I like feeling full and satisfied, and I often pursue that fullness as if it's my right. The idea of giving up food voluntarily feels counterintuitive, maybe even a little unreasonable. But when I've stepped into the discipline of fasting, I've realized how deeply it challenges not just my body but my soul. It exposes how much I rely on comfort, routine, and instant gratification. Fasting is a reset button, a way to confront the idols we didn't even realize we'd built—our appetites, our desires, and the false sense of control we cling to. Paul's words in Philippians 3:18-20 hit hard:

"Their god is their belly... but our citizenship is in heaven."

When my stomach grumbles and my mind races to justify an exception—just a small snack, maybe—I'm reminded of how easily I can become governed by my cravings. Fasting shines a spotlight on these moments, revealing the inner tantrums I throw when I don't get what I want. It's humbling, really. My stomach, my desires, and my so-called rights are dethroned, and I'm faced with a choice: Will I let God be God, or will I cling to these temporary satisfactions?

Fasting also reframes urgency. So often, life feels frantic—decisions to make, deadlines to meet, conversations to have—but fasting reminds me that urgency is often an illusion. In a fast, as my body quietens, my spirit becomes more attuned to heaven's pace. Paul's call in Romans 12:1 to *'present your bodies as a living sacrifice'* takes on new meaning. This isn't just about skipping a meal; it's about offering my entire being—my hunger, my comforts, my control—as a sacrifice to the Lord. It's about declaring that my body, including my stomach, belongs to Him.

And then there are those moments, like walking into a meeting where everyone else is eating pizza. The smell is tantalizing, and my mind instantly starts negotiating with my resolve. But fasting redirects my focus from what I'm giving up to the deeper purpose: to realign my heart with God, to repent, to return to my first love. It's not about punishment or deprivation; it's about dependence. It's about laying down my self-reliance and asking God to renew my mind and spirit.

Ultimately, fasting crystallizes truths like Philippians 3:8-10:

"Everything else is worthless when compared with the infinite value of knowing Christ Jesus my Lord... I want to know Christ and experience the mighty power that raised Him from the dead."

Fasting is a declaration that I want Him more than I want pizza or comfort or control. It's a way of saying, "God, you can have everything, even my appetite."

In dying to myself, I pivot, and I gain something infinitely greater—intimacy with Christ, alignment with His purposes, and the joy of knowing Him more deeply. So, try fasting once in a while.

3. Reevaluate Your Goals.

Maybe the plan you had wasn't the ultimate destination. Take inventory of what still matters and what you can adjust. What's one small, realistic step you can take today to move forward? Standing before the ruin of our home, felled by the massive oak tree, I was struck by how drastically our family goals had to shift for the coming months and perhaps even years. The place of work and ministry that had been our foundation for the past 23 years was no more. It forced an abrupt change in our goals and job descriptions. As daunting as these changes were, they brought into sharp focus the constancy of our ultimate aims. Despite the upheaval, our commitment to becoming more like Jesus, joining in His mission, loving each other deeply, and continuing to learn and grow remained resolute. These core aims became our guiding light through the chaos, reminding us that while circumstances might force us to adjust our goals and plans, our deeper purposes stay steady and true.

Reevaluating our goals doesn't necessarily mean abandoning them. Think of it as goal-enhancing, not goal-replacing. Can you tweak them? Add some sparkle? Subtract the unnecessary? Our current challenges could turn out to be our goals' personal trainers, pushing them to be sharper, stronger, and more refined. If you desire to lose weight by a certain deadline, the core mission is really health. The deadline might shift, but your commitment to health is steadfast. Flexibility in timelines or goals is okay (often even necessary if a deadline change is forced upon you by external forces) as long as your drive remains steady. Regularly check in to ensure you're still on the right track, even if the path changes. View challenges as opportunities to adjust and refine your goals instead of roadblocks. Life's tough moments are your cue to reassess and pivot.

4. *Find Community.*

Growing up in Germany, I was practically handed a manual on self-reliance before I could walk. While knowing how to put on your own socks, matching them with the right shoes, and brushing your teeth with military precision are undeniably life skills worth having, in my case, this self-reliance training came with a side of overachieving perfectionism. In German schools, they don't just hand you a box of pencils—they insist you color-code them, sharpen them to an exact point, and align them with a ruler. By the time you hit kindergarten, you're already living by a detailed daily schedule that rivals a NASA launch plan. Order, structure, and precision are deeply ingrained in the German psyche. While these traits can help you thrive, they also have a way of tricking you into thinking you're entirely self-sufficient.

But here's the thing: self-reliance alone can only take you so far. Sure, you might be able to build a perfectly alphabetized bookshelf or keep your house spotless, but when life throws curveballs that can't be tidied up or scheduled away, you need something more. True resilience—lasting resilience—isn't fueled by our ability to micromanage ourselves into perfection. It's built on dependence: dependence on our Creator and on the people He's placed in our lives. Jesus summed it up perfectly:

"Love the Lord your God with all your heart and with all your soul and with all your mind... and love your neighbor as yourself"
(Matthew 22:37-39).

Self-reliance often whispers the lie that you don't need anyone else, that you can face the storms of life alone. But isolation only weakens us. Resilience grows not in the sterile, solitary bubble of self-sufficiency but in the messy, beautiful web of faith and community. Self-reliance might help you organize your pencils, but it's trust in God and love for and from others that will keep you going when the world feels like it's falling apart. So, by all means, brush your teeth, wear matching socks, and stick to your schedule—but don't for a second think that's enough to build the kind of strength that weathers the storms of life. Don't isolate yourself. Lean on trusted friends, mentors, and a faith community to help you navigate and pivot in the pain. Ecclesiastes 4:9-10 says,

"Two are better than one... If either of them falls down, one can help the other up."

5. *Bring Your Pain And Your Questions To God.*

The God of the Bible is not intimidated by our questions or our lack of clarity—He welcomes them. In fact, the Scriptures are filled with people who struggled with doubt, confusion, and questions, yet God met them in their uncertainty. From the moments of wrestling with faith to the times of raw vulnerability, God's response was not to reprimand but to guide, reveal, and gently correct. Consider the example of Job, who, in the midst of unimaginable suffering, dared to question God's justice and the reasons behind his pain. Rather than silencing him, God responded with a profound dialogue about His sovereignty and the mystery of His ways (Job 38-42). In the New Testament, Thomas, often called "Doubting Thomas," is another example of how God invites our questions. Though he struggled with doubt after Jesus' resurrection, Jesus did not reject him for his uncertainty but invited him to examine His wounds and believe (John 20:24-29). God is not afraid of our doubts. He uses them as opportunities for deeper revelation and faith. We just need to come to Him with our struggles, questions, and doubts.

Questions and doubts aren't just normal—they're often necessary in our attempt to pivot in the pain. They can serve as God's "divine relocation program," as Peter Enns calls it in his book *The Sin of Certainty*,[27] moving us from complacency to deeper truth. We must learn to embrace the unresolved and even allow our doubts to simmer, trusting that they can lead us to deeper understanding and, ultimately, greater trust in Jesus. Without the courage to keep learning and asking, we risk the arrogance of believing we've got it all figured out—and that's a dangerous place to be. The Apostle Paul even describes his own growth in knowledge, saying in 1 Corinthians 13:12,

"For now, we see only a reflection as in a mirror; then, we shall see face to face. Now I know in part; then I shall know fully, even as I am fully known."

Even Paul, one of the most learned and Spirit-filled men in history, acknowledged that his understanding was incomplete and that he would only see things fully in the fullness of time. The unexamined life, a life without continual questioning and growth, leads to complacency and, ultimately, to spiritual stagnation.[28] Spiritual stagnation is the greatest threat to our ability to adapt, grow, and pivot in the face of life's challenges. The danger of

---

[27] Enns, P. (2016). *The Sin of Certainty: Why God Desires Our Trust More Than Our "Correct" Beliefs.* HarperCollins.
[28] **Stagnation:** Lack of growth, development, or movement.

thinking we have it all figured out is that it closes the door to the transformative process of being conformed to the image of Christ (Romans 8:29). By remaining teachable and continually walking with God, we avoid the pitfall of self-reliance and maintain the openness necessary for spiritual maturity. A resilient faith is one that asks questions, seeks deeper understanding, and humbly submits to God's wisdom, knowing that He is the source of all clarity.

6. Act With Faith.

When the oak tree crushed our house and our ministry and community unraveled, we were paralyzed—frozen by the weight of loss and uncertainty. For a while, it felt impossible to think beyond the wreckage. But life didn't pause for us. Decisions had to be made, and we had to move forward, even if all we had in our hands were a few loaves and a couple of fish. Acting in faith meant trusting that God would multiply what little we had to offer. It was agonizing to step away from what we'd known into something unknown and uncertain, but stagnation wasn't an option. With three young kids depending on us, we couldn't afford to stay still.

So, we took the next steps, small as they seemed. As missionaries, we wrote letters to our supporters, inviting them to pray with us and stand in faith for provision. We made phone calls to keep people in the loop. We turned our temporary housing into a cozy refuge, creating as much normalcy as we could for our family. My wife dedicated herself to homeschooling our children while I poured myself into ministry wherever I could. At the same time, we didn't deny our grief. We sought counseling, embraced intentional times of debriefing, and allowed space to process the deep pain of what we'd lost.

A wise man once said, "So many people want to tell God what is on their heart … I have spent my whole life just finding out what is on God's heart and doing it." This simple yet profound truth points us to the greatest treasure we possess here on Earth: our fellowship with the Living God. When we talk about resilience, it's easy to think of strategies or mindsets, but ultimately, no method is as powerful or enduring as a deep relationship with Jesus. To grow resilient is to align our lives with His heart—seeking to understand what He values and what He desires, and then obeying that, acting on it, even when it leads us down difficult paths. This obedience doesn't shield us from tragedy; rather, it equips us to endure it. Walking with Jesus through life's trials teaches us to sing a chorus in the chaos, a melody of faith that resonates beyond our own lives, echoing into the nations and joining the voices of the saints. Resilience isn't born of self-preservation or grit alone; it's born of surrender—a surrender to God's purposes for us and for His world. Only in this active surrender can we find the strength to endure, the courage to hope, and the joy to sing, even in the storm. Even when you can't see the whole picture, take one step forward. You don't have to know the entire plan, but you can trust the One who does. Choose an action that aligns with God's promises, even if it feels small. Go. Move. Do something. Faith doesn't ignore the struggle; it presses forward through it, trusting that God will guide the steps and provide along the way.

7. *Develop New Rhythms.*

Sometimes, pivoting well means creating new habits or letting go of old routines that no longer serve you. Whether it's carving out time for rest, pursuing a creative outlet, or finding new ways to serve others, small shifts in your daily life can lead to significant transformation over time. Change is the one constant we can count on, yet ironically, it's also the thing we often resist the most. Let's face it: most of us would rather cling to the familiar, even when it's no longer working than embrace the uncertainty of something new. We love our routines, our little systems, our "this-is-how-I-do-life" boxes, and when those boxes get flattened by the unexpected—say, a global pandemic or, hypothetically, a giant oak tree crushing your house—it's easy to feel paralyzed.

Take COVID-19, for example. Remember all the hopeful chatter about "going back to normal?"

Spoiler alert: normal never came back, and it probably never will. Instead, we had to figure out how to live in the new normal, which, let's be honest, felt more like learning to juggle while riding a unicycle on a tightrope.

For me, once I've built my little framework for functioning, stepping outside it feels like trying to play a board game without the instructions. It's uncomfortable, messy, and a bit overwhelming. And honestly, sometimes developing new rhythms feels like abandoning who you are. You feel untethered, insecure, and, let's not sugarcoat it, downright awful. Growth hurts. It stretches you, makes you question yourself, and often demands more than you think you have to give. Nonetheless, I'm learning—sometimes the hard way—that the ability to pivot isn't just a nice skill; it's survival. When your house gets flattened by an oak tree, and your work life is thrown into total chaos, you realize pretty quickly that sticking to the old ways just won't cut it. Pivoting isn't about rejecting who you are; it's about adapting to who you're becoming. It's about finding new rhythms that work in the midst of the mess, allowing you to thrive in a world that rarely stays still. Sure, it's painful, and yes, it feels like you're groping around in the dark at times, but it's also where growth happens—because nobody ever became resilient by staying comfortable.

8. *Rely On The Holy Spirit.*

In this journey of learning to pivot when our plans fall apart, we need to recognize that while inner strength has its value, it is not our ultimate source of power. We won't be able to pivot without His power. When life's pressures mount, our true anchor is not the strength we summon from within ourselves but the grace and power of the Holy Spirit. Often, God allows us to reach the end of our own capabilities, showing us that genuine strength cannot be achieved through sheer will alone. This process of "self-emptying," as Paul E. Billheimer writes in *Don't Waste Your Sorrows*, reminds us: "One is often so full of self that there is little room for more of God. Where this is true, God cannot enter in a deeper reality until there has been a divesting of selfish aims and goals, and utter self-emptying. Usually, this requires disastrous failures."[29] These failures aren't without purpose; they are part of a divine stripping away of our self-reliance so that God's strength can fully fill us.

The heart of resilience is a humble dependence on the Holy Spirit, an openness to His power, and a surrender to His leading. We are resilient not because we've mastered self-reliance but because we've discovered that in our weakness, He is strong. When Jesus ascended into heaven, He made an incredible promise: We would never be alone. Enter the Holy Spirit—God's very presence dwelling within us as believers. The Holy Spirit doesn't just comfort us; He lights up our lives with the glory of Jesus. He

---

[29] Billheimer, P. E. (1977). *Don't Waste Your Sorrows*. CLC Publications.

reveals the truth, guides our steps, empowers us, and helps us see through the fog of life's challenges. Sometimes, what we need isn't more time but more power. That power comes through the Holy Spirit.

So, lean into Him. Enjoy His presence and fellowship every day. Seek Him out with bold prayers. Tell Him you desire His power and presence to be fully alive in your life. He's not distant—He's with you and in you, ready to guide and empower you. Romans 8:14 reminds us,

> *"For those who are led by the Spirit of God are the children of God."*

Don't just know about the Holy Spirit—live in His fullness.

Moving Forward

When we pivot in chaos, we align ourselves with God's creative work. He doesn't just patch up broken things—He makes all things new (Revelation 21:5). To pivot is to say, "This pain will not define me. It will refine me." It is to partner with God in His redemptive mission, allowing the broken pieces of our lives to become part of His beautiful mosaic. Pivoting isn't easy. It requires humility, courage, and faith. But as we adjust our plans and surrender to God's greater purpose, we find that life's most challenging moments can lead to its most profound transformations. The road ahead may not look like the one we envisioned, but it is paved with opportunities for growth, resilience, and a deeper reliance on the One who walks with us through every twist and turn.

Pause... Breathe... Reflect.

1. What current challenge are you facing that might require a pivot instead of just perseverance?
2. Is your identity tied to your ability to control outcomes or to your willingness to adapt?
3. Have you mistaken stubbornness for strength? What would it look like to surrender and pivot with purpose?

Word of God Speak

Proverbs 3:5-6

"Trust in the Lord with all your heart and lean not on your own understanding; in all your ways submit to Him, and He will make your paths straight."

Chapter 2
E – Embrace Joy In Uncertainty

Matthew J. Van Natta, in *The Beginner's Guide to Stoicism*, offers a profound insight: "If you want to build up the stable, good passion called Joy, you can't rest your happiness on things that can be taken from you or on future things that may never be."[30] This principle aligns deeply with the teachings of Christianity and finds its ultimate fulfillment in Christ. The Stoic practice of reflection offers a powerful tool for resilience, as it encourages us to regularly review our thoughts, actions, and intentions with an eye toward growth. Marcus Aurelius said, "The happiness of your life depends upon the quality of your thoughts." Reflecting daily gives us a chance to assess and elevate the quality of our thoughts, actions, and responses, allowing us to build a more robust mental and emotional foundation and, in turn, embrace joy even in uncertain times. By taking time each day to consider what went well, what fell short, and what needs further attention, we create a pattern of intentional improvement that enhances our contentment, joy, and resilience over time. Reflection isn't about perfection but

---

[30] Van Natta, M. (2019). *The Beginner's Guide to Stoicism: Tools for Emotional Resilience and Positivity.* Sourcebooks, Inc.

about facing the day's challenges with honesty and humility, learning from them, and preparing for what lies ahead.

While Stoic ideas on reflection can be beneficial, Christianity offers something even more powerful: the opportunity for transformation through a relationship with Jesus. Unlike Stoicism,[31] which encourages self-reliance, Jesus offers guidance, hope, and grace beyond what human effort can achieve. Through prayerful reflection, we are not just processing thoughts or improving self-discipline; we're seeking God's presence and wisdom and asking for His strength. As we review our day, we can bring our successes and shortcomings to Him, allowing His grace to work within us.

A practical way to incorporate this reflection is to take a few minutes before sleep to prayerfully think about the day. What did you do well that you can celebrate? Where did things fall short, and what can you learn from those moments? Was something left undone that you can take care of tomorrow? Instead of carrying the weight of unmet expectations or unfulfilled tasks, release them to God and trust that tomorrow will bring new mercy and strength. In this way, reflection paired with prayer brings both resilience and joy, fostering growth that goes beyond Stoic self-sufficiency to a

---

[31] **Stoicism:** A philosophy promoting self-control and emotional strength.

life transformed by God's love and wisdom.

Stoicism teaches us to detach from the transient and uncertain, recognizing the fragility of worldly possessions and circumstances. My family had to learn that firsthand when that giant oak tree destroyed most of our home. Christianity takes this further by offering a joy that is not merely about detachment but about attachment—to Jesus, the unchanging and eternal source of life. Unlike the Stoic pursuit of inner tranquility through self-reliance, the joy and resilience found in Christ come from dependence on Him. In John 15:11, Jesus says,

"I have told you this so that my joy may be in you and that your joy may be complete."

Jesus doesn't sugarcoat it, doesn't tiptoe around it, and certainly doesn't talk in circles about the reality of life. He's refreshingly, almost startlingly, honest: life will be difficult. Expect challenges of all shapes and sizes, He says. Think of it as His way of saying, "Hey, buckle up—it's not always going to be smooth sailing." But here's the twist: Jesus doesn't just leave us clutching our seatbelts. He speaks directly into those messy, chaotic, heart-wrenching moments of uncertainty, not with hollow platitudes, but with a game-changing promise. He offers His strength—not the "maybe it'll help" kind, but the kind that moves mountains, calms storms, and turns despair into hope. And not just strength to grit your teeth and endure, but strength to embrace joy. Yes, joy! The audacity of it, right? To find peace and purpose when the world feels like it's on fire. Yet, that's precisely what Jesus does. He equips us to rise above, to smile in the storm, to sing a chorus in the chaos. He's not just our Lord and Savior; He's a joy whisperer in the middle of life's wildest rides.

True joy is not in things that can fade or fail but in the unshakable promise of His love, grace, and presence. While Stoicism seeks to master circumstances, Christianity invites us to surrender to a Savior who walks with us, giving us resilience not just to endure life's trials but to overcome them with hope and peace that surpass understanding.

Here are seven thoughtful questions to help you reflect on where your joy truly lies and what it is built upon:

1. ***What am I most afraid of losing, and how would that loss affect my sense of joy and peace?***

Fear often highlights where our joy is rooted. If losing a job, relationship, position, or possession would devastate us, it's a sign our resilience might falter under those circumstances. True resilience begins when we anchor our joy in something eternal, like God's love and promises, which cannot be taken away. Matthew 6:19-20 reminds us to store treasures in heaven, where they are secure. Building resilience means detaching our peace from what's temporary and learning to trust in the unshakable character of God.

2. When I feel happy, what circumstances, possessions, or achievements are contributing to that feeling?

If our happiness is tied to external wins—a promotion, recognition, or comfort—our resilience will waver when those things disappear. Reflecting on this question helps us shift our focus to internal joy, which comes from gratitude and God's faithfulness. As Philippians 4:11-13 teaches, resilience grows when we learn to be content in every situation, finding strength not in what we have but in who sustains us.

3. If all my comforts were stripped away, what would still bring meaning and hope to my life?

True resilience is tested in loss. Would joy remain if all comforts vanished? The apostle Paul endured hardship but found meaning in Christ, calling everything else "garbage" compared to knowing Him (Philippians 3:8). Resilience grows when we root our lives in eternal truths, not fleeting pleasures or possessions. This kind of joy allows us to stand firm, knowing that even in the darkest moments, God's purpose for us remains intact (Romans 8:28).

4. Do I find joy in simply being in God's presence, or does

my joy depend on answered prayers and favorable outcomes?

Resilience is strengthened when our joy isn't tied to circumstances but to God's unchanging presence. If we depend on specific outcomes, setbacks will shake us. Psalm 16:11 says, "In your presence, there is fullness of joy." Resilience grows when we practice gratitude for who God is, regardless of what He does. That is true worship. It allows us to endure trials with a steady heart, knowing that His presence is our ultimate reward.

5. *When trials and challenges come, what do I turn to first for comfort and encouragement?*

Building resilience means examining our default response to difficulty. Do we numb the pain with distractions, or do we draw strength from God? James 1:2-3 tells us to find joy in trials, for they produce perseverance. Resilience grows when we face challenges head-on with trust in Jesus, allowing God to shape our character. By turning to Him first, we learn to weather life's storms with grace and confidence.

6. *Am I more focused on pursuing personal success and happiness, or do I find joy in serving and loving others selflessly?*

Resilience isn't built through selfish ambition but through

selfless love. Jesus demonstrated this when He served others, even in His hardest moments (John 13:14-15). When we prioritize helping others, we shift our focus from our own struggles to a larger purpose. This outward focus fosters resilience, reminding us that we're part of something greater than ourselves and that joy grows when shared.

7. *How often do I remind myself of the eternal hope found in Jesus, and does this hope influence how I experience joy?*

Resilience thrives on hope, and nothing provides greater hope than the promise of eternity with Christ. 1 Peter 1:3-4 reminds us that we have an inheritance that can never perish. Reflecting on this eternal hope fuels resilience, enabling us to face life's trials with confidence. When we fix our eyes on God's unchanging promises, our joy becomes unshakable, and our capacity to endure and overcome grows exponentially.

Prime Yourself for Joy

Priming[32] is a powerful psychological tool that shapes how we perceive and respond to the world around us. Psychologically, priming influences our mindset by activating specific neural pathways[33] and conditioning our brains to focus on specific

---

[32] **Priming (psychological):** Preparing the mind or body for a certain response.
[33] **Neural pathways:** Connections in the brain that strengthen with repetition.

patterns, emotions, or expectations. For example, when we intentionally focus on gratitude or strength before facing a challenge, our brains are prepped to filter incoming stimuli through those lenses. Physiologically, priming affects our body's responses, engaging the autonomic nervous system to either calm or activate us.

When we prime with positive and empowering thoughts, our heart rate stabilizes, stress hormones like cortisol decrease, and neurotransmitters associated with well-being—such as dopamine and serotonin—are released. This state of readiness enhances problem-solving, emotional regulation, and resilience, and it ultimately brings joy. Priming doesn't change external circumstances, but it radically transforms how we experience and engage with them. It is like setting the sail before a storm; you may not control the winds, but you can control how you catch them.

Romans 12:9–21 offers a treasure trove of Biblical priming examples that can recalibrate our hearts and minds, setting us on a resilient, Christ-centered path each day. For instance, *"Hate what is evil; cling to what is good"* (v. 9) primes us to reject toxic thoughts and pursue what is honorable, noble, and true. *"Be joyful in hope, patient in affliction, faithful in prayer"* (v. 12) shifts our perspective from panic to prayerfulness, from despair to enduring hope. Verse 14, *"Bless those who persecute you,"* helps us prepare in advance to respond to conflict with grace rather than retaliation. *"Rejoice with those who rejoice; mourn with those who mourn"* (v. 15) primes our hearts to be empathetic and present with others, increasing our emotional resilience and relational depth. Finally, *"Do not be overcome by evil, but overcome evil with good"* (v. 21) sets a daily intention to respond to challenges with kindness and integrity rather than anger or fear. By intentionally reflecting on these truths and inviting the Spirit's help to live them out, we can prime ourselves for lives marked by peace, joy, and unwavering resilience in Christ.

Here are some practical steps to prime yourself toward joy and resilience and learn to embrace joy in uncertainty:

1. *Morning Declaration and Prayer:* Start your day with worship. Recognize the goodness and power of God within you. Use intentional words. Speak truth and hope over your upcoming day—declare who you are and what you are capable of in Christ.

2. *Controlled Breathing:* Spend 2–3 minutes practicing slow, deep breathing to calm your nervous system and focus your mind.

3. *Visualization:* Picture yourself responding calmly and confidently to challenges that might arise. Imagine your resilience and joy growing with each step forward.

4. ***Gratitude Practice:*** Write down or reflect on three things you're grateful for. Gratitude shifts your brain from fear-based thinking to abundance and possibility.

5. ***Set a Mental Anchor:*** Choose a word or phrase (e.g., "Steady," "Strong in Him," "Resilient") and repeat it throughout the day to center your thoughts when you feel overwhelmed.

6. ***Physical Movement:*** A brief walk, stretching, or exercise primes your body and mind by increasing blood flow and releasing endorphins that boost mental clarity and resilience.

These practices may seem small, but over time, they create mental and emotional muscle memory for resilience. Priming helps you build an internal reservoir of strength, making it easier to respond thoughtfully, courageously, and perhaps even joyfully when life throws the unexpected at you.

Pause... Breathe... Reflect.

1. Are you chasing temporary happiness or cultivating lasting joy rooted in something deeper?
2. What if uncertainty isn't the enemy of joy but the soil in which it grows?
3. Can you name a time when joy surprised you in the middle of a storm? What did that teach you?

Word of God Speak

Habakkuk 3:17–18

"Though the fig tree should not blossom... yet I will rejoice in the Lord; I will take joy in the God of my salvation."

Chapter 3
R – Reframe

There was a season when I had to completely rethink what it really means to be a man — a full-on reframe of my entire perspective on masculinity. You know, those moments when you feel like you're falling short in the "manly" skills department — like fixing cars, hunting, fishing, or even just knowing which end of a wrench to use. I had the grunting down, sure, but when it came to the rest, I was as lost as a cow on AstroTurf.

I vividly recall a day when I was mowing the lawn, and the mower suddenly conked out. I yanked that starter cord like I was trying to start a fighter jet, but it stubbornly refused to roar back to life. Frustration took the wheel, and I did what many of us do when life doesn't go our way — I got angry. I hollered for Marsha, my wife, the unsung hero of many a household crisis, who came out and took one look at the mower.

"Have you checked the spark plug?" she asked, almost casually, like it was the most obvious thing in the world.

"The what?" I replied, feeling the familiar sting of incompetence.

Marsha walked over, unscrewed the spark plug, gave it a little tap, blew on it like a Nintendo cartridge, and screwed it back in. "Try it now," she said. I gave the cord a pull, and like a resurrection on a Saturday afternoon, the mower roared to life.

In that moment, I felt about as manly as a soggy washcloth. Nothing takes the wind out of a man's sails quite like the realization that he might actually be useless when it comes to the practicalities of life. That moment made me question myself. It made me question my manhood.

Thankfully, as the years have passed, I've come to see that true masculinity isn't about mastering every skill, like hunting, shooting, or fixing things. It's about grappling with the weight of responsibility, facing our failures, and finding the strength to keep going when we feel inadequate. Real manhood, and for that matter, real personhood, isn't defined by a skill set. It's forged in the messy process of becoming, sharpened by teachability and resilience, and proven by showing up even when you don't have all the answers. It's about surrendering your heart to Jesus, embracing self-control, and cultivating empathy. Skills and abilities are valuable (and I'm learning as I go), but they don't define your worth. True manhood is found in the depth of your character — in your ability to love sacrificially, lead with integrity, and serve others with humility.

Fatherhood has been another nonstop, mind-bending

rollercoaster of reframes. Just when you think you've got it all figured out, one of your kids throws you a curveball (sometimes literally) that leaves you scratching your head, bandaging your knee, or repairing a shattered window. It's taught me how to negotiate with a tiny human who thinks they're the boss, how to fix a broken toy with nothing but duct tape and sheer determination, and how to be a leader even when I feel completely unqualified.

As a father, my ultimate goal is to equip my kids for life's wild journey — to help them succeed, love deeply, laugh freely, cry healthily, and face suffering with resilience. I want them to walk with Jesus, encouraged, rooted in wisdom, grace, empathy, and forgiveness, guided by a deep understanding of God's love and purpose. That's the mission I've signed up for when I became a dad. But was I even remotely prepared for the nonstop reframing required in my own heart and mind to actually pull this off? Not even close!

During my kids' formative years, I've uttered "I'm sorry" to them more times than I can count. Truth is, if I can't own up to my mistakes and shortcomings, if I can't say sorry, I'll miss out on truly impacting my kids. Hopefully, my frequent apologies have shown them that teachability and humility go a long way. So, dads, relax, say you're sorry, and hug your kids as often as possible (while they still let you). Becoming a dad reshaped my entire perspective more than anything else ever could. It redefined my priorities, rewired my instincts, and reframed how I see the world.

One night, I was tucking in my girls, Julia and Vivian. The house was quiet, the kind of stillness that feels sacred after a long day. I sat on the edge of their beds, brushing my hand gently through their hair, watching their little chests rise and fall. There's something profoundly humbling about those moments — watching your children rest peacefully, unaware of the storms you're navigating as an adult.

As I sat there, my heart whispered a prayer: "Father, you've got them?" It wasn't just a question but a plea, a release, and maybe even a little parental fear wrapped in hope. In that stillness, before my doubts could creep in, I sensed God's response as clear as day: "I've got them!" Not a vague assurance or a passing sentiment, but a deep, soul-anchoring promise.

I am deeply grateful for my walk with Jesus, especially in my fragility as a dad, husband, and just as a man navigating the chaos of life. I've come to realize that when I bring my disappointments, unmet expectations, and brokenness to Him, He doesn't just help me survive the storm. He reframes and restores, redirects and comforts, teaches and strengthens, reshaping my perspective and giving me the resilience to become who He's called me to be. He takes what feels shattered and turns it into something whole, transforming mess into meaning. Prayer and the presence of God are the greatest resources we have for a true reframe. I'm genuinely excited about this chapter as we dive deeper into the power and necessity of reframes in our lives.

Soccer and a Profound Perspective Reframe

My son played soccer for most of his childhood, and for the first few years, I was his coach. Eventually, though, he got too good, and we moved him to play club soccer. I didn't mind trading my whistle for a car key because those countless hours driving to practices, games, and tournaments became something special. The tournaments, especially, meant long car rides filled with music and chatter about the latest Lego set or his new favorite soccer move. But every now and then, those car rides took a deeper turn. I remember one conversation vividly. We were reflecting on some mistakes—his, mine, life's little blunders. With a thoughtful sigh, Samuel mused, "Wouldn't it be nice if we could travel back in time and erase our mistakes?" I paused, considering how appealing that idea sounded. But as we talked it through, we realized that trying to undo mistakes could unravel so much more, potentially creating a whole new set of problems. We laughed at the irony and eventually concluded, "Rather than erasing our mistakes, let's just learn from them." And there it was—a profound perspective reframe. Life's not about avoiding mistakes; it's about owning them, growing through them, and becoming better because of them.

It's always worth pausing to reflect on how much our unconscious assumptions shape how we see the world. These hidden beliefs about what is true and real act like invisible lenses, influencing how we interpret everything. Most of the time, we don't even realize how much these assumptions confine our thought patterns and how greatly a reframe would help us. What if we took a moment to challenge those assumptions? What if we allowed ourselves to consider possibilities beyond our current way of thinking? While some things are open to change and growth, it's important to remember that certain truths are non-negotiable and don't need a reframe. Just as blue will always be blue, 1+1 will always equal 2, and Jesus will forever be the King of kings. These unshakable realities provide the foundation for everything else to grow and be framed. I'm not talking about these non-negotiables. I'm talking about ways of thinking, operating, relationships, perspectives, hopes for the future, ingrained routines, and methods that could benefit from being questioned, evaluated, and reframed.

Imagine if you could go back and tell your younger self one piece of wisdom—how different would things look? And now flip it—what would your future self say about the situation you're stuck in right now? Once I've established a framework or a system that works, I struggle to even entertain the idea that there might be something better outside of that familiar comfort zone. I don't know if comfort zone is the right word here. I have always been okay with discomfort, conflict, and the occasional workplace friction. I suppose you could say that I wasn't necessarily pursuing comfort but consistency. Pursuing consistency is a good thing if consistency remains a means to an end and not the thing that sustains you.

When that framework, consistency, and familiarity are threatened, it's like my mind hits a wall, unwilling to consider that growth might require stepping out of what feels safe and established. The challenge, then, is learning to see beyond the boundaries we've unknowingly set for ourselves and to open up to new, perhaps even better, ways of seeing and living. I often need to learn to value the process of reframing my perspective.

As followers of Jesus, our ultimate purpose is to become more like Him. Yet, in the busyness of life, I often find myself striving to make sense of everything, searching for solutions, organizing my world, and building frameworks that help me function. In doing so, it's easy to lose sight of the main goal: why I'm really here. The purpose of all change, all pivoting, and all reframing is not self-actualization. It's about something far deeper: strengthening my relationship with Jesus. Every shift in life, every challenge or blessing, is an opportunity to draw closer to Him. Jesus didn't just come to provide for us or make our future better—though He does care for us deeply—He came to bring our hearts into His presence. Our pursuit is not about chasing miracles or success but deepening our relationship with the One who created us. At the end of the day, the most important thing is not whether life is perfectly organized or comfortable but whether our hearts are at home in His presence. That's the real miracle, and that's what He calls us to seek above all else.

Marriage and family therapist Nicole Zasowski, in her remarkable book *What If It's Wonderful*, writes: "Our expectant hearts become demanding hearts when our delight in Christ is contingent upon God giving power to our plans. I once heard an idol described as anything in which the outcome has the power to change our view of Christ."[34] This strikes at the core of our faith journey: Does our joy and worship depend on how our story ends, or are we truly following Jesus regardless of the outcome? Are we content if God's provision doesn't align with our personal vision? These are hard questions; for someone like me, who tends to find comfort in established frameworks and systems, they cut even deeper. I've always thought I could handle change, but the reality is some changes are incredibly difficult. Am I so focused on

---

[34] Zasowski, N. (2022). *What If It's Wonderful?: An Invitation to Release Your Fears, Choose Joy, and Find the Courage to Celebrate*. Thomas Nelson.

preserving my own ways of doing things that I'm missing out on what God really wants to do in my life? This reflection challenges us to surrender and reframe, trusting that God's plans, even when they disrupt our own, are far better.

Learned Optimism

When hardships hit, it's so easy to see them as permanent, letting them define our future. We feel them as pervasive, affecting every part of our lives. And worst of all, we take them deeply personal, as if they're a reflection of our worth. But what if they're not the whole story? What if they're just a chapter, not a conclusion?

Martin E. P. Seligman's *Learned Optimism*[35] is a foundational work in positive psychology that explores how our explanatory styles—how we interpret and explain events—shape our outlook on life and our overall mental health. Seligman's work highlights the transformative power of reframing, specifically shifting from a pessimistic mindset to an optimistic one. He argues that while pessimism is often learned, optimism can be cultivated through intentional practice, improving resilience, productivity, and well-being.

---

[35] Seligman, M. E. (2011). *Learned Optimism: How to Change Your Mind and Your Life.* Vintage.

Seligman identifies three key dimensions of explanatory style:

o Permanence: Optimists view setbacks as temporary, while pessimists see them as permanent.

o Pervasiveness: Optimists isolate failures to specific situations, whereas pessimists generalize them across all areas of life.

o Personalization: Optimists externalize blame for negative events when appropriate, while pessimists internalize it, often leading to feelings of helplessness or unworthiness.

These dimensions determine how individuals react to challenges and setbacks. A pessimistic explanatory style, characterized by beliefs like "This will never get better," can lead to learned helplessness[36]—a state in which people feel powerless to change their circumstances. Conversely, a reframed and more optimistic explanatory style can foster resilience and a proactive approach to problem-solving. Seligman's early experiments with dogs demonstrated how repeated exposure to uncontrollable adverse events led to learned helplessness. When the dogs were later placed in situations where escape was possible, they failed to act because they had internalized the belief that their actions would not make a difference. Humans exhibit similar behaviors when

---

[36] **Learned helplessness:** Feeling stuck and not even trying to change because you believe nothing will help.

they adopt a defeatist mindset after repeated failures or hardships.

According to Seligman, optimism is not a naive denial of reality but a choice to reframe and interpret events in a way that fosters hope, action, and resilience. Optimistic people experience better physical and mental health, achieve greater success, and form stronger social connections.

Seligman outlines practical strategies to unlearn pessimism and embrace optimism, primarily through cognitive reframing[37] techniques. The ABC model (Adversity, Belief, Consequence) encourages individuals to identify and challenge irrational beliefs that arise in response to adversity, replacing them with more constructive and accurate interpretations. At its heart, *Learned Optimism* is a call to reframe how we interpret life's challenges. Seligman's work reveals that our explanatory styles are not fixed; they can be reshaped through intentional effort. This aligns with the idea that we all occasionally need a reframe, especially when life becomes overwhelming or disorienting.

For example, imagine someone experiencing a career setback, such as being passed over for a promotion. A pessimistic perspective might interpret this as a permanent failure ("I'll never advance in my career"), pervasive ("I'm not good at anything"),

---

[37] **Cognitive reframing:** The mental practice of looking at a situation from a different perspective to change how one feels about it.

and personal ("I'm not smart enough"). Such a mindset can lead to discouragement and inaction. However, by reframing the experience through the lens of optimism, the individual can see the setback as temporary ("This is just one promotion"), specific ("It doesn't define my entire career"), and external ("There may have been other factors at play"). This shift enables them to take constructive steps forward, such as seeking feedback or pursuing additional training.

After the collapse of our ministry and the departure of nearly everyone we had served alongside, we were suddenly without work. I applied for several jobs that aligned well with my gifts and how I could best serve. Rejection, however, doesn't sit easily, does it? Each "no" felt personal, like a critique of my identity and worth. It began to seep into how I viewed other areas of my life—areas that hadn't really been an issue suddenly seemed insurmountable.

One thing had nothing to do with the other, but I couldn't see it at the time. After a few rejections, it was hard not to believe this was permanent, that doors would keep closing indefinitely. My tendency for extremes only amplified the situation, taking emotions and setbacks to places they didn't need to go. I desperately needed a reframe—a shift in perspective and a renewed trust in Jesus—to avoid getting stuck in the quicksand of self-pity.

It felt like a test of resilience, a muscle I hadn't exercised enough. Resilience isn't automatic; it's a choice. Eric Greitens captures it well: "You weren't born with resilience, any more than you were born with the ability to use a compass or aim a rifle. Resilience is an excellence we build. We can practice it in the choices we make and the actions we take. After enough practice, resilience becomes part of who we are."[38] That hit home. I had to consciously decide not to let these setbacks define me. I had to choose to trust the Lord again, to reframe what was happening. This wasn't personal—they simply chose someone else. This wasn't permanent—it was a temporary season. And one setback in one area of life didn't need to bleed into every other area. Slowly but surely, I learned to see these rejections as moments of growth, opportunities to trust God more deeply, and to build the resilience that would carry me forward.

Seligman's work is a powerful reminder that while we can't control everything we experience, we can control how we interpret those experiences. We can pay attention to the language we use to explain challenges. Are you falling into the trap of permanence, pervasiveness, or personalization? As Christians, reframing isn't just about positive thinking—it's about anchoring our thoughts in God's truth and our trust in Him. By doing so, we gain a hopeful

---

[38] Greitens, E. (2015). *Resilience: Hard-Won Wisdom for Living a Better Life.* Houghton Mifflin Harcourt.

outlook and the strength to face life's trials with faith and resilience.

Reframing Begins With Asking Questions

In every season of life, ask yourself, "What can this teach me? How can this change me?" Shifting from victimhood to a growth mindset[39] doesn't minimize the pain but empowers you to move through it. Find ways to see challenges as opportunities for personal and spiritual growth. Let's face it—this process is complicated, often painful, and anything but joyful, but here's an unpopular opinion: the goal of life isn't just to feel good or to be perpetually happy. Resilient people get this. They understand that life is complex and involves a broad spectrum of emotions, each with its purpose. To be truly resilient, we need to fully feel these emotions, not ignoring or numbing them but reframing them and not letting them rule over us.

1. Is It Time To Reframe How I Understand Joy And Happiness?

Happiness, in particular, has been lifted up as the ideal emotional state, but if happiness isn't where we are today, that doesn't mean we've failed. It's perfectly possible, even necessary, to experience tough, heavy, or even plain "off" days without

---

[39] **Growth mindset:** Belief that abilities can improve through effort.

labeling them as setbacks. When we reframe our perspective, we begin to see that each feeling — joy, grief, anger, peace — can serve as a stepping stone toward growth. Resilient people know this truth: becoming more like Jesus is a journey that inevitably includes the painful parts, the dry seasons, and the days when "happy" feels out of reach. Our growth doesn't come from a smooth, unchallenged life but from the ability to reframe our perspective, persevering through the ups and downs, and learning to navigate each experience without being swept away by it. While the world may push for a "feel-good" life, reframing our perspective gives us resilience, which teaches us to lean into life as it is, not merely as we wish it would be.

The concept of the hedonic treadmill[40] explains why people, no matter how much they achieve or acquire, often find themselves back at their baseline level of happiness. It's the constant chase for more—more comfort, more security, more of what we think will finally make us feel settled—that keeps us running but never arriving. We long for stability because it gives us control in a chaotic world. For me, this desire for stability expresses itself in my deep reliance on established frameworks. These frameworks— whether they are routines, roles, or familiar environments—are my safe spaces. They create boundaries where I know how to operate,

---

[40] **Hedonic treadmill:** The idea that people quickly get used to good or bad changes and return to the same level of happiness.

allowing me to feel competent and secure. But when these structures are threatened, I feel helpless, unmoored, and exposed. I don't like feeling helpless, and when I do, my instinct is to overcompensate by clinging even tighter to those expired frameworks, treating them as if they're still the best place for me, even when they no longer serve my growth.

This tendency can trap me in old patterns and keep me from embracing new opportunities that God might be placing in my path. It's like being stuck on that hedonic treadmill, holding onto past certainties even as they slow me down or hold me back. This overcompensation often becomes a way of avoiding the discomfort of change, a way of pretending that I'm still in control when, in reality, things are shifting beyond my grasp. It's hard to admit that what once worked is no longer working; it's even harder to trust that stepping off the treadmill—letting go of expired systems— isn't a loss but an invitation to something better. Stability is good, but not when it becomes a prison of our own making. The challenge is to recognize when our desire for control is keeping us stuck and to have the courage to trust that, even in the instability, God is doing something new and calling us to grow beyond the frameworks we've built for ourselves.

The hedonic treadmill is the idea that no matter how much we achieve or how many good things we get, we quickly get used to them and return to our usual level of happiness. It's like running on a treadmill: you keep moving forward but never really get anywhere. Whether it's a new job, more money, or the latest gadget, we always end up wanting more, and our happiness doesn't increase for long. It shows why chasing after things doesn't bring lasting joy because we quickly adapt to whatever we have and start looking for the next thing.

2. Is It Time To Reframe How I Relate To The Past?

While we were in Germany visiting my family in the summer of 2024, my dad pulled out an old photo album filled with pictures from when I was just 11 years old, back when he and I went hiking in the Alps. Seeing those photos more than 30 years later was a surreal experience. It stirred up emotions as I tried to recall those moments from so long ago. But as I looked through those images, I realized I needed to reframe my perspective. I couldn't allow myself to slip into regret and melancholy or start thinking, "Why didn't I enjoy that time more with my dad? Did I waste it!" Such thoughts would only haunt me, filling me with unnecessary sadness. Remembering the past is valuable, but becoming trapped in a past you cannot change is a burden that serves no purpose. It's a reminder that while it's good to reflect, it's essential to keep moving forward without letting regret overtake the present.

Nostalgia, often seen as a comforting reminder of the past, can sometimes become a dangerous trap that distorts our perceptions of the present and robs us of resilience. Our memories are not as reliable as we might think, and we often need a reframe. They are often colored by emotions and time, leading us to idealize certain moments while forgetting the challenges that accompanied them. For example, when older people tell young parents to "treasure every moment because it goes so fast," they may be overlooking the stress, exhaustion, and struggles that come with parenting. This well-meaning advice can create pressure to feel perpetual joy in an inherently complex and difficult situation. While the intention is to help young parents appreciate the fleeting nature of childhood, it can inadvertently gloss over the real and valid emotions of fatigue and frustration. This selective memory is not just a benign quirk; it can foster a sense of melancholy and longing that paralyzes us in the present, causing us to yearn for an idealized past rather than fully engage with the realities of today. Clinging to romanticized reminiscence weakens resilience; true strength is built by reframing our perspectives and embracing the present.

Holding on too tightly to certain emotions or experiences from the past can even be harmful, creating emotional hooks that anchor us to bygone days and prevent us from moving forward. Acknowledging our emotions—whether good, bad, or ugly—is an essential part of emotional health, but once we have processed and worked through these feelings, it's crucial to release them. Holding on too tightly can lead to regret, perceived missed opportunities, and a life lived in the shadow of "what could have been." Instead, it's healthier to accept gratitude for what was and then turn our attention to what lies ahead. As Ecclesiastes 3:1 reminds us,

"There is a time for everything and a season for every activity under the heavens."

This biblical wisdom encourages us to fully embrace each season of life without clinging to the past or fearing the future. The key is to recognize that life is a series of adventures, each with unique challenges and joys. When one adventure ends, it's time to embark on the next with hope and anticipation rather than being bogged down by what has already passed. Every day is a new opportunity, a fresh start given to us by God's mercy, which is *"new every morning"* (Lamentations 3:23). This is a powerful antidote to the paralyzing effects of nostalgia, melancholy, and regret. Life is meant to be lived actively, not passively. This forward-focused mindset builds resilience, encouraging us to continually adapt, reframe, grow, and embrace the present rather than getting stuck in the past.

3. Is It Time To Reframe How I Relate To The Present?

Another reframe we need to undertake is the angst of the present. Ever since I was a kid, I've grappled with the uneasy feeling of whether I'd be provided for. Spoiler alert: being a missionary hasn't exactly helped. I could be sitting down to a hearty meal under a solid roof, with a car in the driveway, yet still be consumed by the dread of "What if the well runs dry tomorrow?" Throw in the extra anxiety about the world's myriad crises, and it often feels like I'm a single drop in an ocean of turmoil. There's this nagging sensation that no matter how much I do, I'm barely scratching the surface of making a difference. It's like being equipped with a squirt gun to tackle a forest fire. But maybe, just maybe, if we can reframe these fears and uncertainties, we can see them for what they really are: opportunities for faith and growth rather than insurmountable obstacles.

When we attempt to shoulder the weight of all the world's problems, we can become paralyzed by the sheer enormity of the task. In today's age, we are bombarded with constant negative news, amplifying our awareness of global issues and blurring the lines between what we can control and what we cannot. This incessant exposure can overwhelm our minds and hearts, making distinguishing between genuine callings and burdensome distractions difficult. We might feel compelled to engage in every battle and fix every wrong. Yet, such an approach can lead to burnout and disillusionment. Jordan Peterson's affirmation, "We may well be incapable of tending the whole world, but we can manage our own small private natural spaces, and that is far from nothing,"[41] reminds us of the importance of focusing on our manageable spheres of influence—our own small private spaces. We cultivate resilience and purpose by acknowledging our limitations, dependence on God, and prioritizing our efforts. In these moments of clarity, we can genuinely contribute to the world, not through grandiose gestures but by faithfully tending to the responsibilities and passions that align with our capacity and calling. Resilience isn't about doing everything; it's about doing what truly matters.

Let's talk about time for a moment—a relentless, no-nonsense force that doesn't hit the brakes for anyone. Time is unstoppable, unyielding, and completely indifferent to our pleas for a pause button. When you're young, it's easy to shrug it off. After all, you've got "forever" ahead of you, right? But as the years stack up and you've weathered some storms—hardships, loss, those "why did I do that?" moments—you start to realize something. Time doesn't negotiate. It doesn't rewind. Every choice you made, every word you spoke, every step you took is cemented in the past. Yesterday is out of your hands. Done. Finished. But enter the reframe and realize that today isn't. Sure, you're a day older, but (hopefully) you're also wiser. So, the real question isn't about yesterday—it's about right now, today. What are you going to do

[41] Peterson, J. B. (2024). *We Who Wrestle with God: Perceptions of the Divine.* Random House.

today to make it count?

4. *Is It Time To Reframe How I Relate To The Challenges I Face?*

Resilience, not permanent damage, is the norm regarding human experiences. Though I'm not a psychologist, and I don't claim to fully understand the complex inner workings of someone who has faced deep trauma, I do know this: as a father, my deepest desire is to equip my kids with resilience and to overcome limiting beliefs about themselves, God, and the world around them. We live in a world that seems intent on removing every obstacle, challenge, and danger from a child's path, but that doesn't build strength. Taking competition out of soccer games or padding every playground doesn't create kids who are ready for life's unpredictable and often harsh terrain. Real growth doesn't come from avoiding hardship; it comes from facing it.

Imagine welding training wheels to a child's bike, giving them a temporary sense of achievement. Sure, they can pedal faster, but they'll never be ready for the bumps and twists of a real ride. Like that terrain, life is full of challenges, and without the opportunity to fail, how will they ever learn to navigate it? Kids and young adults need the freedom to struggle, fall, and regain themselves. Only through failure do they learn how to stand stronger. In those moments of hardship, resilience is born—when we allow them to face challenges rather than protect them from every possible setback. Resilience is forged in the real world, not in a bubble-wrapped version.

5. *Is It Time To Reframe How I Relate To The World Around Me?*

Emotional and social intelligence are like secret weapons for reframing the world around you in a positive light. Think of emotional intelligence as your internal compass, helping you recognize, understand, and manage your emotions instead of letting them run the show. It keeps you from spiraling into despair after a tough day. It allows you to reframe challenges as opportunities to grow. Social intelligence, on the other hand, is your external superpower—the ability to navigate relationships and understand the emotions of others. When you combine these two, you're equipped to shift perspectives for yourself and those around you. Instead of letting conflict escalate, you can steer it into understanding. Instead of wallowing in self-doubt, you can identify the encouragement in someone's kind words. Emotional and social intelligence gives you the tools to rewrite the narrative, helping you see setbacks as setups for comebacks and turning relational tensions into teachable moments.

As men, husbands, and fathers, we often crave the grand gestures—the heroic moments where we step in and save the day.

We imagine ourselves taking a bullet for our families without hesitation. Yet, the simple, daily acts of love feel like an impossible ask. Taking out the trash? Interrupting work to settle another round of sibling squabbles? These tasks feel beneath the epic narrative we want for our lives. I struggled to learn that loving my family means embracing the mundane. I thought I was made for more, not realizing how selfish that pursuit was. It was high time to reframe how I related to the world around me. Real life isn't a Hollywood action movie filled with unattainable heroism. It's made up of showing up every day, dethroning self, and fighting for others—especially those we love most.

And here's another irony: as men, we often struggle to restrain our anger but think we can lead an army. We imagine ourselves as great warriors, but our real strength is leading with patience, humility, and love at home. True heroism isn't in dramatic sacrifices but in the quiet, consistent ways we serve and love. The battlefield we're called to isn't always out there; often, it's right in our living rooms. Winning at home, in the little things, is the most meaningful victory of all. Generally, people react to setbacks, crises, and chaos in various ways, but two of the most common responses are anger and self-pity. While these emotions may feel justified, they are two of the greatest enemies of building resilience. Dealing with this often requires a major reframe. Anger can consume us, keeping us in bitterness, while self-pity convinces us that we're helpless victims of circumstance. Both emotions act like a prison, locking us into cycles of unforgiveness, preventing healing, and holding us back from moving forward. The Bible warns us about the dangers of unchecked anger:

"Be angry, and do not sin; do not let the sun go down on your anger and give no opportunity to the devil" (Ephesians 4:26-27).

Similarly, self-pity leads us away from gratitude and faith, which can harden our hearts. Proverbs 14:30 reminds us,

"A heart at peace gives life to the body, but envy rots the bones."

Self-pity, rooted in comparison or despair, eats away at our resilience just as envy does.

Matthew 6:14-15 encourages us to forgive (ourselves and others), recognizing that holding onto grudges binds us to the past. Psalm 37:8 advises us to reframe and *"refrain from anger and forsake wrath! Fret not yourself; it tends only to evil."* By releasing anger and choosing hope, you open the door to resilience, allowing yourself to move forward in faith.

Reframing is a Journey

Reframing our perspective is a transformative journey that demands intentionality and patience as we learn to reset our minds and align our hearts with God's truth. It's not an overnight fix but a purposeful process, like realigning a lens to bring a blurred image into sharp focus. Start with rest—not just physical rest, though that's crucial, but soul-deep rest in God's unchanging love. Think of Elijah under the broom tree, utterly spent and needing nourishment and restoration before he could hear God's gentle whisper (1 Kings 19:5-6). Rest isn't a luxury; it's the foundation for clarity.

Once your soul begins to quiet, identify the issue. Don't shy away from asking hard questions. What's cluttering your perspective? Negative thoughts, disappointments, unrealistic expectations, or old patterns that need breaking? Name them. Acknowledging the need for reframing is half the battle, and it's often in stillness and wise counsel that clarity begins to emerge (Romans 12:2-3).

Anchor your soul in Scripture. God's Word is the ultimate corrective lens, replacing the lies we believe with the unshakable truth of His promises. Memorize verses that speak to your situation (Psalm 119:11) and meditate on them. Picture God's Word as the north star, steady and guiding when everything else feels chaotic. Journaling can help you process these reflections—pouring your heart onto the page can reveal God's fingerprints in places you hadn't noticed before (Philippians 4:8). Write honestly, but also record moments of gratitude and growth to reflect on when the journey feels uphill.

Prayer is your lifeline to renewal. Invite the Holy Spirit to reshape your thoughts, illuminate your understanding, and deepen your trust in the Father's love (Ephesians 4:23-24). As you pray, be specific. Ask God to transform particular areas of your thinking and open your eyes to the ways He's already working. Remember, this isn't a solo mission. Seek guidance from wise counselors or mentors who can offer perspective and wisdom that you might lack at the moment (Proverbs 11:14). Their encouragement can be a divine gift, pointing you toward hope and healing.

Gratitude is another key practice. When life feels overwhelming, gratitude can shift your focus from what's wrong to what's right. It doesn't mean ignoring difficulties but acknowledging the ways God is still good and faithful in the midst of them (1 Thessalonians 5:18). Gratitude is like a magnifying glass—it helps you see blessings that were always there but overlooked.

Finally, put your reframed perspective into action. Cherish it. Serve others with humility and joy. When we take our eyes off ourselves and look to meet the needs of others, we often find that our perspective is being reframed. We gain purpose in the process (Galatians 5:13). Don't let setbacks discourage you. Challenges aren't roadblocks; they're opportunities to learn and grow. Celebrate the small victories—the moments when you see progress, even if it's just a little. Trust that God faithfully completes the good work He started in you, even when you can't see the full picture yet (Philippians 1:6).

Reframing isn't about perfection. It's about progression—taking intentional, grace-filled steps toward seeing your life, your circumstances, and your God with fresh eyes. It's a pathway to healing, growth, and an unshakable trust in Jesus, who promises to walk with you every step of the way.

Order Out of Chaos

Scott Walker's *Order Out of Chaos*[42] explores how we can bring clarity, structure, and meaning to life's messiest moments. Walker's premise is straightforward yet deeply profound: the chaos in our lives is not inherently destructive; rather, our interpretation determines whether it erodes us or shapes us into something stronger. Walker argues that our power lies in reframing the meaning we assign to events, and his insights challenge readers to take ownership of their emotional responses and reactions to life's disruptions.

This hit home for me recently during a seemingly innocuous moment—cooking stir fry on my grill. I'd carefully prepared all the ingredients, visualized the perfect meal, and set everything in

---

[42] Walker, S. (2023). *Order Out Of Chaos: A Kidnap Negotiator's Guide to Influence and Persuasion.* The Sunday Times bestseller. Hachette UK.

motion. My son Samuel, however, requested to grill a small piece of chicken himself. While this should have been a bonding moment, it irritated me because it disrupted my plan. My grill wasn't heating evenly, two slices of cucumber fell to the ground, and before I knew it, my carefully orchestrated plan turned into frustration, anger, and—if I'm honest—an emotional meltdown over a stir fry. In hindsight, this overreaction was absurd, but in the moment, it felt uncontrollable.

What Walker might say here is that I gave in to my internal narrative, and I desperately needed a reframe. When the falling cucumbers, among other things, interrupted my plan, I assigned the event the meaning of failure and chaos, and my emotional reaction followed that interpretation. Instead of asking empowering questions like "So what?" or "Now what?" I spiraled into a narrative of irritation, allowing my emotions to dictate my behavior. Walker's wisdom reminds us that the meaning we assign to events determines our emotional response. The stir fry wasn't the problem—my interpretation of the moment was.

Walker emphasizes that while we can't always control the chaos, we can control the lens through which we view it. This principle is liberating. He challenges us to slow down, reframe, and even become aware of the language we use to describe situations. For example, instead of saying, "Everything's ruined," we could say, "Okay, this didn't go as planned, but what can I learn from it?" or "Is this really such a big deal deserving of such a strong response?" By reframing and shifting our language, we shift our emotional trajectory.

Reflecting on this, I've realized that my empathy often shuts down when plans derail, and my mind races to fix what feels broken. If fixing it seems impossible, I default to anger. Walker points out that this pattern erodes resilience because it traps us in a reactive loop rather than empowering us to reframe and respond constructively. I've seen this not only in my grill debacle but also in more profound moments, like grappling with the emotional fallout of our ministry collapsing.

Walker's book resonates because it's not about avoiding chaos but about partnering with it. He offers practical strategies for reframing our experiences: asking better questions, evaluating the meaning we assign to events, and developing emotional agility. For me, this has meant learning to pause, breathe, and ask, "What's really happening here?" It also means examining the language I use when describing situations, ensuring it reflects truth rather than exaggerated emotion. Walker teaches that the power is in the reframe and that power lies with us.

Resilience is not just about enduring difficulties; it's about developing the presence of mind to navigate challenges with clarity and creativity. When faced with problems that don't have immediate solutions, one of the most critical tools we can utilize is controlled breathing. Breathing regulates our physiological state, calming the amygdala[43]—the part of the brain responsible for fight-or-flight reactions—and enabling the prefrontal cortex, our center for rational thinking, to engage fully. When we don't overreact but instead pause, slow our breath, and allow ourselves to process the situation, we unlock a deeper capacity to think critically and creatively. Overreaction narrows our perspective, creating tunnel vision that blinds us to potential solutions.

On the other hand, resilience encourages us to embrace uncertainty, stay calm, and approach challenges with a sense of curiosity rather than panic. Consider Joseph in the Bible: when thrown into a pit by his brothers and later imprisoned unjustly, he didn't collapse under the weight of the chaos and the unknown. Instead, he leaned on God, stayed composed, and used his God-given wisdom to interpret dreams and offer solutions that elevated him to positions of influence. Similarly, by cultivating emotional regulation and intentional problem-solving, we create space to see opportunities where others might only see obstacles. Resilience doesn't guarantee immediate answers, but it ensures we remain steadfast and resourceful as we search for them.

---

[43] **Amygdala:** The part of the brain that handles emotions like fear.

Life will always throw uneven grills, fallen cucumbers, and moments of genuine, profound upheaval our way. But the real challenge is in learning to reframe, to respond with grace rather than mere reaction, and to find meaning that leads to growth, not despair. As Walker puts it, the meaning is ours to assign—so choose wisely.

Pause... Breathe... Reflect.

1. What story are you telling yourself about your current situation—and is it the only possible interpretation?
2. Are you giving God enough time to finish the picture before declaring what the situation means?
3. What mindset shift might unlock peace or perspective in your current struggle?

Word of God Speak

Romans 12:2

"Do not conform to the pattern of this world, but be transformed by the renewing of your mind..."

Chapter 4
S – Strengthen Relationships

In his groundbreaking book, *The Boy Who Was Raised As A Dog*,[44] Dr. Bruce D. Perry develops the idea that children aren't born resilient. They are made resilient. It has always been strange to me when adults attribute resilience to children as if it's something innate, a quality they're born with. I recall a conversation with a dad who had just confessed to cheating on his wife and was seeking a divorce. His young daughters were understandably devastated by his decision. His response? "Oh, they'll bounce back. Kids are so resilient." This notion never sat well with me. Resilience isn't a default setting in children; it's cultivated. It's nurtured by parents and other influential adults who create environments where children can safely make mistakes, experiment, think creatively, experience failure, and be comforted and guided through it all. All our relationships matter. Children aren't rubber balls that simply bounce back after being thrown against the wall of life. They're delicate souls who need love, attention, support, and guidance to develop true resilience. Our

---

[44] Perry, B. D., & Szalavitz, M. (2017). *The Boy Who Was Raised As A Dog: And Other Stories from a Child Psychiatrist's Notebook—What Traumatized Children Can Teach Us About Loss, Love, and Healing.* Hachette UK.

responsibility as adults is to provide them with the tools and the space to grow resilient, be there to catch them when they fall and help them rise stronger each time.

A home that is safe, consistent, and somewhat predictable lays the groundwork for children to flourish. It sets the stage for an environment where they feel secure enough to let their imaginations run wild, to take the leap into the unknown, and to start sculpting their own identities. When kids have a stable and nurturing home life, they're more inclined to develop confidence, resilience, and a strong sense of self. This sense of security emboldens them to tackle challenges head-on, learn from their missteps, and evolve into resilient and adaptable individuals. In essence, safe and stable relationships at home provide the canvas upon which children can paint the picture of who they want to be. It's the launchpad for their dreams, the sanctuary where they can retreat and regroup, and the foundation upon which they can build a bright and promising future.

Dr. Perry writes: "Through moderate, predictable challenges, our stress response systems are activated moderately. This makes for a resilient, flexible stress response capacity. The stronger stress response system in the present is the one that has had moderate, patterned stress in the past."[45] In simpler terms, when children encounter manageable challenges, their bodies and minds learn to adapt and respond effectively to stress. This process is akin to physical exercise; just as lifting weights builds muscle strength, facing challenges builds resilience in handling stress. For mom and dad, this highlights the responsibility of providing an environment where children can experience these moderate challenges. It means allowing them to face age-appropriate difficulties, such as learning new skills, navigating social situations, or dealing with minor setbacks. However, it's important that these challenges are not overwhelming or traumatic, as this can have the opposite effect and lead to maladaptive stress responses.[46]

Dr. Perry goes on: "The more healthy relationships a child has, the more likely he will be to recover from trauma and thrive. Relationships are the agents of change, and the most powerful therapy is human love ... Fire can warm or consume, water can quench or drown, wind can caress or cut. And so it is with human relationships: we can both create and destroy, nurture and terrorize,

---

[45] Perry, B. D., & Szalavitz, M. (2017). *The Boy Who Was Raised As A Dog: And Other Stories from a Child Psychiatrist's Notebook—What Traumatized Children Can Teach Us About Loss, Love, and Healing.* Hachette UK.
[46] **Maladaptive stress response:** a harmful or ineffective way of dealing with stress that may create new problems instead of resolving the underlying issue.

traumatize and heal each other."[47]

Dr. Perry's profound insight aligns with timeless biblical principles that underscore the centrality of relationships and the transformative nature of love. Throughout the Bible, we find numerous verses that highlight the significance of healthy relationships in our lives. Proverbs 17:17, for instance, proclaims, *"A friend loves at all times, and a brother is born for a time of adversity,"* emphasizing the enduring nature of love and support in our relationships, particularly during challenging seasons.

The biblical narrative of Ruth and Naomi vividly illustrates the impact of relationships on healing and growth. Ruth's steadfast loyalty to Naomi becomes a source of hope and restoration amid deep loss and hardship. Through their relationship, both women find solace, strength, and purpose. Ruth's story culminates in her inclusion in the lineage of Jesus, highlighting the profound influence of relationships on our spiritual journey (Ruth 1-4).

Applying this principle involves focusing on and investing in meaningful relationships, especially during adverse times. By offering love, support, and companionship to those in need, we begin a chain of healing and transformation in their lives.

---

[47] Perry, B. D., & Szalavitz, M. (2017). *The Boy Who Was Raised As A Dog: And Other Stories from a Child Psychiatrist's Notebook—What Traumatized Children Can Teach Us About Loss, Love, and Healing.* Hachette UK.

Additionally, cultivating healthy relationships within a church community plays a crucial role in our spiritual growth and well-being. Attending church regularly is not just a good idea or some sort of religious obligation; it is an essential component of our spiritual journey and, I'd venture to say, a requirement to fully follow Jesus. It provides us with a supportive community where we can connect with others, experience God together, share our faith, find encouragement, struggle relationally, walk in teachability and openness, and receive spiritual sustenance.[48]

In the context of a local church body, we can grow in our understanding of God's love and purpose for our lives, others, and the world. The church is not just a building; it ought to be a vibrant community of believers who are committed to following Jesus and supporting one another along the way. Our relationship with God is intimately connected to our relationships with others, particularly within the context of a local church body. As we engage in meaningful and, at times, vulnerable relationships and actively participate in a church community, we experience the transformative power of love in our lives and become more fully equipped to follow Jesus faithfully.

Focusing on healthy relationships plays a crucial role in

---

[48] **Spiritual sustenance:** Nourishment for the soul or spirit, often derived from prayer, scripture, or community.

fostering resilience. The Bible repeatedly emphasizes the importance of supportive relationships in times of adversity. Proverbs 27:17 states,

"As iron sharpens iron, so one person sharpens another."

This highlights how positive relationships can strengthen and uplift us, even when sparks fly at times. Similarly, Ecclesiastes 4:9-10 emphasizes the value of companionship, stating that *"two are better than one, because they have a good return for their labor: If either of them falls down, one can help the other up. But pity anyone who falls and has no one to help them up."*

In Renovation of the Heart, Dallas Willard uses a phrase that's lingered in my mind like a stubborn song lyric: we need to have a "well-kept heart."[49] At first glance, it sounds simple, but the more you think about it, the deeper it gets. What are you letting in? What are you nourishing? What weeds of bitterness, resentment, or distraction have crept in and are choking out joy, peace, or clarity? A well-kept heart isn't passive; it's not like a garden that magically blooms without weeding, watering, or pruning. It takes effort, intention, and attention. A well-kept heart isn't formed in isolation and takes community and other people. Willard breaks down the process of cultivating a well-kept heart into intentional practices:

---

[49] Willard, D. (2014). *Renovation Of The Heart: Putting On the Character of Christ.* Tyndale House.

thoughts, feelings, choices, bodies, social context, and soul. Each plays a vital role.

Your thoughts shape your reality—what you dwell on will inevitably shape your heart. Your feelings are the outflow of what's inside. Are they aligned with God's truth or dictated by fleeting circumstances? The choices you make daily—the small, seemingly insignificant ones—are what steer your life in the long run. Are you choosing habits that build steadfastness and resilience now, or are you letting apathy take over? Your body matters too. Willard reminds us that our physical habits, what we eat, how we rest, and even how we breathe affect the state of our hearts.

Then there's the social context. The days leading up to the moment when the giant oak tree hit our house had been soaked in relentless rain, saturating the ground until it could no longer bear the weight of that ancient giant. At times, trees tumble not because their roots are weak but because the soil they're planted in is unhealthy. Even the strongest roots can fail if the soil is eroded, shallow, or full of toxins. The same is true for us. Where we are planted matters. Psalm 1:3 describes the righteous person as *"a tree planted by streams of water, which yields its fruit in season and whose leaf does not wither."* The soil we are rooted in—the spiritual, relational, and emotional environment we cultivate— determines our ability to stand firm and be steadfast when the storms of life hit or when we're challenged in our faith.

Take a moment and ask yourself: who are the people around you? Are they helping you cultivate a well-kept heart that's open, generous, and centered on Christ, or are they pulling you into negativity and complacency? The adage "Show me your friends, and I will show you who you will become" encapsulates a profound truth about human nature and the impact of relationships on our lives. The people we surround ourselves with exert a powerful influence on our thoughts, beliefs, behaviors, and, ultimately, our character. Friends can either uplift us, inspire us to grow, pray with us, and support us in our endeavors, or they can lead us to negativity, worldliness, complacency, and stagnation. The company we keep shapes our values, shapes our aspirations, and shapes our worldview. Therefore, it is crucial to choose our friends wisely, seeking out those who share our values, love Jesus, encourage our growth, and challenge us to be the best versions of ourselves.

The Good Life

In *The Good Life*,[50] Robert Waldinger, M.D., and Marc Schulz, Ph.D., take readers on an illuminating journey through the findings of the longest-running scientific study on human

---

[50] Waldinger, R., & Schulz, M. (2025). *The Good Life: Lessons from the World's Longest Scientific Study of Happiness.* Simon and Schuster.

happiness: the Harvard Study of Adult Development. Spanning over 80 years and multiple generations, the study has meticulously examined what makes life truly fulfilling. The answer is not wealth, fame, status, or professional success—it is relationships. Deep, meaningful connections with others are the single most significant factor in determining long-term happiness, resilience, physical health, and overall well-being.

At its core, the book reinforces a simple yet often overlooked truth. Who we surround ourselves with determines who we become. Relationships shape our mental and emotional well-being, influence our habits and choices, and even impact our longevity. The study found that people with strong, supportive relationships lived happier lives and were physically healthier, with lower rates of heart disease, depression, and cognitive decline. Conversely, loneliness and social isolation were linked to increased stress, chronic illness, and even premature death.

Waldinger and Schulz argue that having good relationships is only part of the equation; being a good friend, partner, and community member is just as crucial. It's not enough to accumulate people around us—we must actively invest in those relationships. Good relationships require presence, intentionality, and the willingness to show up for others in both the joys and struggles of life.

One of the most compelling insights from the study is that the people we consistently engage with mold our character, beliefs, and habits. Just as iron sharpens iron, the quality of our friendships and relationships determines the kind of person we become. Toxic or shallow relationships deplete us, while uplifting and supportive relationships strengthen our resilience and character.

This means we must be intentional about who we allow into our inner circle. Are we surrounded by people who inspire us, hold us accountable, and push us toward growth? Or are we entangled in relationships that drain our joy and reinforce destructive patterns? The book challenges us to take stock of our relationships and cultivate environments that nurture and refine us.

While much emphasis is placed on finding good relationships, Waldinger and Schulz highlight that true fulfillment comes not only from receiving love and support but also from giving it. We must strive to be the kind of friend, spouse, or family member that we would want in our own lives. This means being reliable, practicing empathy, listening deeply, and showing up when it matters.

Too often, people focus on getting friendships rather than investing in them. Relationships require effort, and those who make that effort—who check in on friends, express appreciation, forgive quickly, and prioritize connection—are the ones who ultimately experience the richest and most satisfying lives.

Practical Takeaways: How to Cultivate a Good Life

Waldinger and Schulz offer several practical strategies for building and maintaining meaningful relationships:

- Prioritize people over productivity. In a world obsessed with busyness, it's easy to let relationships take a backseat. But true happiness comes from connection, not achievement.
- Be intentional in friendships. Don't just wait for relationships to happen—nurture them. Schedule time with friends, initiate conversations and express gratitude.
- Surround yourself with people who inspire you. Choose relationships that challenge you to grow, deepen your faith, and reinforce the kind of person you want to become.
- Be the friend you want to have. If you want more love, encouragement, and support in your life, start by offering it to others.
- Embrace vulnerability. The deepest relationships require honesty and the willingness to share our true selves. Don't be afraid to open up.

- Resolve conflicts with grace. Holding grudges poisons relationships. Approach difficult conversations with humility and a desire for peace.
- Invest in long-term connections. Friendships and marriages don't last without effort. Keep showing up, even when life gets busy.

At the core of a resilient and well-kept heart is a profound but simple truth: the strongest, healthiest people are not those who accumulate the most success, money, or possessions but those who cultivate deep, life-giving relationships. Who we surround ourselves with shapes not only our happiness but also our resilience, emotional well-being, and personal growth. And while finding good friends is essential, being a good friend is just as important.

In a world increasingly driven by digital connection yet plagued by loneliness, we must recognize that resilience is not built in isolation. It thrives in community, through friendships, and in the support of those who walk alongside us. If we want to grow stronger in life's challenges, we must prioritize people—loving well, showing up, and intentionally investing in the relationships that sustain and refine us.

Pause... Breathe... Reflect.

1. Who are the people you can lean on when life gets heavy—and are you leaning in?
2. Are you only seeking support or also offering it? Who might need your presence right now?
3. What does true community look like in your life, and where is it lacking?

Word of God Speak

Ecclesiastes 4:9–10

"Two are better than one... If either of them falls down, one can help the other up."

Chapter 5

P – Perspective Over Perfection

When my son, Samuel, was just a little tyke, I recall a day that felt like a whirlwind in the Langer household. It was one of those days when everything seemed topsy-turvy, and our to-do list was longer than the Mississippi. To make matters worse, my wife and I were not exactly in sync. I was gearing up to run an errand, already feeling frazzled, when my wife hollered, "Take Samuel with you!" So, I scooped up my little champ and marched him out to the car with all the enthusiasm of a grumpy bear. Buckling him into his car seat felt like wrestling a greased pig—it's always a twisted mess, no matter how many times you straighten it out. If I ever cross paths with the genius who invented children's car seats, I've got a bone to pick with them! As I muttered under my breath, trying to fasten the seatbelt, Samuel suddenly exclaimed, "Papa, look at the leaf!" I was so wrapped up in my frustration that I didn't quite catch what he said at first. "What was that, Samuel?" I asked, still preoccupied. With even more delight in his voice, he repeated, "Look at the leaf. It's dancing!" Intrigued, I turned around, and sure enough, there was a lone leaf gracefully twirling and pirouetting its way down from the tree. Samuel was completely enchanted by this simple moment, and it hit me like a ton of bricks—I almost let my anger and impatience steal this precious moment and a precious connection with my son from me.

Kids have this remarkable way of reminding us about the beauty of the simple things in life. Parenting, as challenging as it can be, has taught me invaluable lessons and given me the privilege of watching my children grow into amazing individuals. Don't miss the leaf!

In today's world, we are constantly distracted from deliberately weaving the tapestry of our lives and are bombarded with information from every direction—social media updates, news alerts, endless streams of emails, and more. This deluge of data can overwhelm our senses and dilute our perspective, leading to what someone aptly described as a "poverty of attention." To build resilience, it's essential to tune into both our inner life and the world around us. The sheer volume of information we are confronted with each moment demands that we prioritize our attention, selecting what's truly important and filtering out the noise.

This necessity to prioritize is not just about managing distractions; it's about intentionally choosing to focus and gain true perspectives. By consciously directing our attention to the areas that matter most—whether it's spending time with Jesus, nurturing relationships, pursuing personal growth, or dedicating ourselves to meaningful work—we can achieve a deeper sense of fulfillment, resilience, and effectiveness. Perspective over perfection. Don't miss the "leaves of life." Share your joys with God, and let Him share in your celebrations. Bring your challenges to Jesus, let Him alter your perspective where needed, and guide you through difficult moments. If we make this a daily practice, even with the small things, we will be better prepared when tragedy strikes. Prioritizing our attention allows us to weave purposefully, and to invest our cognitive and emotional energy wisely, ensuring that we are not merely reacting to the world but proactively shaping our lives. Therefore, by prioritizing our attention, we create the life we desire, filled with purpose and clarity even amidst the chaos.

Life is Extremely Intricate

At just 20 years old, I left my home in Germany, setting out on a journey that would take me across continents and through countless experiences. I've stood before congregations as a worship leader, guided others as a pastor, and served as a missionary, carrying the message of the Gospel to the far corners of the world. I've had the privilege of ministering to and leading many along the way. But for all the miles traveled, lives touched, and lessons learned, I'm acutely aware that I am very much still a work in progress. Every step of this journey has shaped me, my perspective, and worldview, but the journey is far from over.

Perspective over perfection—that's the name of the game. We're all walking construction zones, complete with the occasional detour, pothole, and "work in progress" sign flashing above our heads. Our perspectives aren't fixed; they're constantly being molded by our experiences, relationships, and even the mistakes we'd rather forget. Perfection? It's a myth, a mirage in the desert of self-improvement. Progress, though—that's where the gold is. It's not about nailing every decision or always getting it right. It's about stepping back, recalibrating, and asking, "What did I learn?" Growth happens when we focus less on having a flawless finish and more on refining the lens through which we see the world, allowing God to lead us. Perspective keeps us moving forward, not stuck chasing a perfection that doesn't exist. After all, the journey is the masterpiece, not the destination.

I am writing this book not from some religious ivory tower but from the trenches of life, where I've faced battles and been wounded, humbled, and shaped by numerous challenges. I'm writing this book from a place realizing that life is extremely intricate. It is a beautifully complex tapestry woven with countless threads—relationships, ambitions, challenges, triumphs, setbacks, dreams, and the daily demands that vie for our attention. It's a whirlwind of experiences, each one shaping and refining us in unique ways. Yet, within this multifaceted journey, having focus and perspective is fundamental. Without focus, the complexity of life can quickly turn overwhelming, scattering our energy in too many directions and leaving us feeling lost, without resilience, and stretched thin. Focus and perspective act as our compass, guiding us through the noise and honing our attention on what truly matters—God's kingdom, core values, meaningful goals, and the pursuits that enrich our lives and those around us. With perspective, we can find clarity amid chaos, purpose within our choices, and strength to press on with resilience and determination.

Consider This

Perspective is more than just keeping your eyes on a goal; it's a discipline, a choice, and an anchor that grounds us, especially in life's storms. When distractions pull at us from all sides, focus reminds us of who we are, what we're here for, and how we're going to get there. Resilience doesn't come from trying to do everything but rather from learning to do the right things with a steady heart and clear purpose. Focus and perspective enable resilience, helping us direct our energy into what truly matters rather than being scattered and overwhelmed by the noise around us.

Jesus Himself embodied the power of focus and perspective, setting His face toward Jerusalem despite knowing the suffering awaiting Him (Luke 9:51). He stayed undeterred and single-minded in His mission to bring redemption. This wasn't about a simple act of willpower; it was a model of unshakable focus, which allowed Him to endure unimaginable hardship with resilience and grace. Jesus' ability to remain steadfast and laser-focused on His purpose gave Him the strength to face even the cross.

The Apostle Paul gives us a powerful metaphor for focus in 1 Corinthians 9:24-26:

"Do you not know that in a race all the runners run, but only one gets the prize? Run in such a way as to get the prize. Everyone who competes in the games goes into strict training. They do it to get a crown that will not last, but we do it to get a crown that will last forever."

Paul's words remind us that focused discipline is the way to resilience. Like an athlete training for a race, Paul urges us to focus on what we pursue and to run in such a way that we can endure whatever challenges come our way.

The way we begin our day sets the tone for everything that follows. When we rush into our morning, filled with stress and pressure, our bodies and minds take their cues from that. It's like programming ourselves and our perspective to operate in high-stress mode for the rest of the day, with shallow breathing, a racing heart, and a scattered mind. But what if, instead, we chose to start with calm? Breathing deeply, slowing down our heartbeat, and centering our thoughts on what truly matters? Just as our body needs oxygen to function properly, our soul needs stillness with God to thrive.

The Bible reminds us in Psalm 46:10,

"Be still, and know that I am God."

This is a daily invitation to begin our mornings differently—by going to bed earlier and waking up earlier, creating space to meet with Jesus. Imagine starting each day in prayer, meditation, and intentional breathing, allowing your spirit to be anchored before the demands of life hit. This daily practice doesn't just prepare us for the day ahead. It transforms how we handle stress, ensuring we approach challenges with peace, clarity, and resilience.

Ah, yes, resilience begins when we learn to control the pace of our mornings and surrender them to God's guidance. Picture it: a serene, blissful sunrise, the aroma of fresh coffee filling the air, and a peaceful house where everything is perfectly in order. You quietly sip your coffee while reflecting on your spiritual goals for the day—maybe even reciting some inspirational verses in the calm of the morning. Sounds idyllic, right? In reality, it often looks like this: the kids are yelling from another room, the coffee maker is on strike, and your favorite mug is nowhere to be found. As you're rushing to find a missing shoe, your kids are throwing a tantrum over breakfast choices, and the dog is trying to eat your

Bible (yes, that really happened). Ah, the joy of mornings!

Yes, controlling the pace of your morning and surrendering it to God's guidance is the goal, but let's be honest—it's easier said than done when you're navigating the chaos of real life. However, this is part of the song we've got to learn to sing in chaos. Life is tough, kids are loud, and a toddler's meltdown can derail even the most well-planned morning. The tough truth is that true perspective and resilience aren't built in the calm, picture-perfect moments; they are forged in the messy, loud, and unpredictable moments. Accept them! It's the ability to surrender control and still move forward when everything around you feels out of whack. So, even though it's a daily challenge, it's worth pursuing—because if we can find peace and perspective in the storm (or the cereal spill), we're on our way to building something unshakable. And hey, if all else fails, there's always coffee (once you've fixed your coffee maker).

Perspective also involves knowing what to prioritize—and what to let go. In today's fast-paced world, it's easy to say "yes" to every opportunity, but constantly doing so can dilute our strength. Even Jesus prioritized His time, often stepping away from the crowds to spend time with His Father in prayer (Luke 5:16). He focused on His mission, refusing to be sidetracked by others' demands or societal pressures.

Take inventory of your commitments. Are there things you've said "yes" to that distract you from your deeper goals? Revisit these priorities regularly, and don't be afraid to say "no" to things that may drain your energy or lead you off course. Perspective and resilience are sustained when we're not trying to do everything but when we focus on doing the right things with our full heart and soul.

Colossians 3:2 advises us,

"Set your minds on things above, not on earthly things."

By focusing on what has eternal value, we build resilience that can withstand the shifting values of society and the disappointments of temporary pursuits. Make a habit of reflecting on where you're spending your mental and emotional energy. If there's something that consumes your attention that doesn't align with your values or goals, consider setting boundaries. For instance, limit your screen time or the time you spend worrying about things you can't control. Redirecting your energy to what truly matters strengthens resilience and helps you maintain a sense of peace, even when life feels chaotic. I don't journal often but I have found writing down thoughts and emotions during a difficult time can be extremely helpful. Try journaling your struggles and looking for lessons in them. By focusing on growth rather than simply "getting through it," you'll build resilience and find purpose even in difficult seasons.

The Power of Visualization

Focus and perspective also involve visualizing the future and the person you are becoming. Proverbs 29:18 says,

"Where there is no vision, the people perish."

Visualizing your goals and the life you want to build strengthens your focus and resilience. When you have a clear picture of where you're going, it's easier to press on when things get tough. Also, capitalize on the positive power of negative visualization.[51] Negative visualization is a paradoxical yet powerful tool that equips us to gain true perspective and navigate life's uncertainties with resilience and wisdom. Imagine rehearsing your response to losing a job—not because you expect it, but so you're prepared emotionally and mentally. By considering what steps you'd take, like updating your resume, tightening your budget, or leaning into your network, you're not giving in to fear; you're building a safety net. Or think about a loved one facing a health crisis—envisioning how you might support them can shift your focus from panic to purpose. Even mundane examples, like imagining being stuck in traffic, can help. Instead of frustration, you might plan how to use the time productively, like listening to

---

[51] **Negative visualization:** A technique that involves imagining the worst-case scenario to build emotional resilience.

an inspiring podcast or spending time in prayer. Negative visualization isn't about fixating on worst-case scenarios but transforming "what ifs" into "I can handle this." By mentally walking through challenges, you sharpen your gratitude for what you have, gain clarity about what matters most, and cultivate true and helpful perspectives.

How we perceive the world shapes nearly every aspect of our lives, from our actions to our emotional well-being and even the outcomes we achieve. Our underlying beliefs act as a lens, filtering and coloring our view of reality. When these beliefs align with a sense of purpose and direction, we find that our effectiveness and fulfillment increase. This sense of direction is greatly enhanced when we pursue well-defined objectives—goals that provide focus, meaning, and the fuel for resilience. The power of visualization cannot be underestimated here; the images we hold in our minds help mold our experiences in the tangible world, guiding our steps and influencing the reality we create.

Perspective Shift[52]

In his seminal work *The Obstacle Is The Way*,[53] Ryan Holiday writes, "Perception is personal. You have more control over what

---

[52] **Perspective shift:** A change in the way one thinks, views, or interprets situations.
[53] Holiday, R. (2014). *The Obstacle Is The Way: The Timeless Art of Turning Trials into Triumph*. Penguin.

you believe than you realize." At first glance, this statement seems deceptively simple, yet it reveals a profound truth about the power of perspective. Our beliefs and our perspectives, the lens through which we interpret life's events, are not fixed; they are malleable[54] and subject to change when we are willing to challenge and reframe them. This requires a willingness to unlearn entrenched ways of seeing the world—patterns of thought that may no longer serve us or align with reality. Life, as frustrating and exhilarating as it is, seems to be a never-ending journey from one perspective shift to the next, kind of like upgrading your prescription glasses just when you've finally gotten used to the old pair. Just when we think we've figured things out, some unexpected plot twist, failure, or revelation forces us to tilt our heads, squint a little, and see things differently. It's as if God, in His infinite wisdom (and maybe a little divine humor), refuses to let us get too comfortable in our assumptions. Growth isn't about locking in the "right" way of seeing the world—it's about staying humble and willing to adjust our lenses as we gain new insight. The trick is embracing the shifts rather than fighting them. Because chances are, we're always one perspective change away from the clarity we didn't even know we needed.

Unlearning is as much about humility as it is about growth. It

---

[54] **Malleable:** Able to be shaped or influenced; flexible.

means admitting that our initial perceptions may be flawed or incomplete. It also demands the discipline to remain calm amidst uncertainty or chaos, resisting the instinct to join the collective panic. When others react impulsively, a resilient mind pauses to assess the problem, stripping away emotional noise to identify the core issues at hand. Only then can we begin to seek solutions with clarity and intention. I'll admit it—I can be a hothead. Impulsivity has often hijacked my better judgment, shoving calmness, clarity, and communication into the backseat while my emotions took the wheel. Over the years, I've worked—sometimes successfully, sometimes not—to breathe, step back, and untangle my feelings from the situation. Easier said than done, whether in parenting, leadership, or navigating conflict. I've had to unlearn how to react when I feel attacked—or worse, when others are unjustly targeted.

On the other hand, many people need a perspective shift—not away from conflict, but toward engaging in it wisely. When our ministry unraveled, I felt the weight of my years in leadership and the urgency of the crisis. I raised my voice, calling for action. Some criticized my tone, timing, or delivery. I understand their concerns, but given the gravity of the situation, urgency was necessary. Too often, our discomfort with conflict leads us to dismiss hard truths by focusing on how they're spoken rather than what's being said. Yes, wisdom, restraint, and emotional discipline matter. But so does knowing when to speak with force and conviction—because when injustice unfolds, silence isn't wisdom; it's complicity.

Open the Bathroom Door

I've always been tempted to fall victim when life doesn't go how I think it should. Maybe it's because I don't like feeling helpless—it's uncomfortable, disorienting, and forces me to confront my limitations. When I can't solve a situation or see beyond the immediate problem, helplessness whispers its lies, and I start to think of myself as the victim. That mindset, though, is a thief. It robs me of resilience, closes doors to possibilities, and keeps me stuck in a posture of defeat rather than progress.

And yet, I've struggled deeply with these thoughts. What if I'm forgotten? What if I'm overlooked? What if I won't have enough to survive? What if I fail at what I was put on this earth to do? What if I'm a failure as a dad? These questions don't gently knock on the door of my mind—they storm in, setting up camp in the corners of my heart, whispering that safety lies in clinging to what I have and retreating to a corner. When this happens, I don't fight for the next step—I flee. It's less resilience and more self-preservation, and it leaves me more fearful than fortified.

As I write this, I'm in my mid-forties, and some days, it feels like time is sand slipping through my fingers. I've been arguing with Jesus since my late thirties, telling Him I've reached halftime in life. "Lord," I've said, "if You don't show me soon what You want me to focus on for the next 20 or 30 years, then all of this will have been wasted!" I know it's not the most faith-filled argument, but it's honest. But why do I get so anxious about tomorrow? Why does it feel like tomorrow is lurking around the corner with an "I told you so" ready to brand me a failure?

The truth is, I needed a total perspective shift—an unlearning of how I see myself and the world around me. I don't need to white-knuckle my way through life, nor do I need to shrink back in fear. I need to stop measuring my worth by what I've accomplished or what might happen tomorrow. Instead, I need to trust the One who holds tomorrow, to let Him shape my perspective and show me who I truly am.

There I was, deep in the throes of an existential crisis—sitting on the toilet, of all places (apologies for the mental image). I was lost in thought, contemplating how much I longed to be needed, to be sought after for my wisdom, to be an expert in something—anything—so that people would come to me for advice. Surely, somewhere out there in the vast expanse of human existence, my moment of true significance was waiting. And then, just as I was about to unlock the secrets of my destiny, reality quite literally knocked on the door.

It was my youngest daughter, Vivian, her little voice piercing through my philosophical haze: "Papa, will you come play with me?" I barely registered the request, too consumed by my grand musings.

"Just a minute, I'm in the bathroom," I said, eager to return to my internal search for meaning. And then, like a well-aimed slap from the universe, it hit me—how utterly ridiculous I was being. Here I was, lamenting my desire to be needed and wanted, while an actual human being—a tiny one, no less—was standing outside my door doing exactly that. I was so busy searching for significance in some abstract future that I nearly missed the purest, most tangible form of it standing right in front of me. The irony was almost poetic. That was a harsh but beautiful perspective shift. Turns out, meaning wasn't hiding in some distant, theoretical constellation—I just had to open the bathroom door.

Values, Significance, Trials, and the Power of the Quiet Life

I recently took my family on a getaway to Beavers Bend in Oklahoma, a place where nature stretches out in breathtaking beauty. Among the pine-covered hills and crystal-clear rivers, we visited a museum that recounted the early history of lumber and logging in the area. It was fascinating to learn how the pioneers lived—building simple cabins and working tirelessly to cut wood, one axe swing at a time. These people didn't have smart homes or gourmet meal kits. Their daily victories consisted of keeping their homes weatherproof and feeding their families while laboring in the forests. They didn't agonize over existential questions about purpose or "living their best life." Their lives were rugged but focused, tethered to the earth and their immediate needs. I couldn't help but wonder: Is the endless buffet of opportunities we have today actually better? Or has it made us more restless, more discontent, and ultimately less resilient?

Let me admit something: I would have hated this kind of sentiment in my 20s. Back then, when it felt like the prime of life (spoiler: it wasn't), I was an achiever, a go-getter, a galvanizer. If someone had told me to "seek balance," I would have smiled politely and then ignored them entirely. I understand now that life has seasons, and sometimes balance feels impossible in certain seasons. But here's the truth: resilience through balance is true in every season. In my 20s, it was there—just harder to see. Now, it's more crystalized, the wisdom coming into focus like a sunrise you can't ignore.

Resilience, after all, is squashed when we're perpetually disconnected and unsettled, and when we measure our worth by how far we've climbed rather than how steady our footing is. Perhaps there's wisdom in the apostle Paul's advice to Timothy: to live a quiet life (1 Thessalonians 4:11), mind your own affairs, and find satisfaction in your daily work. For those early loggers, life wasn't about chasing unattainable dreams but about chopping the next tree and making the next meal. And somehow, their grounded simplicity cultivated resilience in ways our overstimulated, achievement-driven world struggles to grasp.

But how do we reconcile this with the 21st-century lifestyle, where endless notifications and global opportunities pull us in every direction? And what about the Great Commission, which calls us to make disciples of all nations? The answer lies, again, in balance. A life devoted to God's mission doesn't have to be frantic or complicated. Jesus Himself lived with purpose yet embraced many quiet moments of prayer and reflection. He taught that God's kingdom grows like a seed, slowly and faithfully (Mark 4:26-29). We can engage with the world while still finding joy in the simple rhythms of life, anchored by contentment and a clear sense of purpose. It's about being present in our everyday tasks, finding meaning in what's before us, and trusting God to multiply our efforts in His time. Isaiah reminds us,

"Even youths grow tired and weary, and young men stumble and fall; but those who hope in the Lord will renew their strength"
(Isaiah 40:30-31).

Maybe resilience isn't found in chasing the stars but in living the quiet, steady, and deeply rooted life God has called us to.

For many years, I failed to grasp the profound power of a quiet life, and the pursuit of significance has consumed me. I sought recognition for my work, in my words and in my actions. I chased after significance, preparing sermons, worship times, and leading in pursuit of being noticed.

Now, as a dad, at times, I caught myself parenting with a desire for personal significance, missing the true essence of parenthood. Truthfully, however, parenting is like juggling flaming torches while riding a unicycle on a tightrope—chaotic, unpredictable, and definitely not the ideal setting for a quest for personal significance. It's more about survival mode than seeking personal glory. So, if you're looking for a calm, orderly path to personal significance, parenting might not be the right gig for you. But if you're up for a wild, unpredictable ride that will challenge you in ways you never imagined, make you into a better person, draw you closer to God, and show you your true values, welcome aboard the parenting rollercoaster!

Parenting has a way of stripping away facades, revealing our deepest motives and it truly is about losing your own sense of importance and giving yourself wholly to another. At times, I've caught myself thinking, "Once my kids are grown, then I can focus on my own significance and redirect my focus to my own aspirations." However, I've come to realize that my greatest impact and significance come from surrendering, serving, and self-sacrificially giving myself to my kids in the present. My values have shifted. It's in the everyday, seemingly mundane tasks of parenting that true significance is forged in the late-night conversations, the shared laughter, and the comforting hugs that most meaning is unearthed. I'm learning that true significance is found in giving my best to my best right here, right now. My kids deserve nothing less. In this journey, I'm discovering that significance is not revealed in what I achieve but in how I love and serve those entrusted to me.

This realization has been both enlightening and challenging for me, particularly because one of my top five values and strengths, according to the StrengthsFinder assessment, is Significance. This strength, when harnessed positively, can drive me to achieve great things and make a meaningful impact. However, if misdirected, it can lead me down a path of seeking personal validation and recognition above all else.

As I'm navigating fatherhood, I'm learning (slowly but hopefully surely) that true significance isn't found in accolades or personal achievements but in the sacrificial giving of oneself for the sake of others, especially my children. This shift in perspective has reshaped how I view my role as a husband, father, pastor, and leader and has helped me prioritize what truly matters in life. I'm very much still on this journey of learning and growth, trying to apply this truth in my daily life. After all, true strength lies in a man's ability to admit when he's wrong, learn from his missteps, and have the resolve to set things right.

As we meander through the twists and turns of life, our values evolve and grow, much like we do. Some values become more defined, while others become more flexible as we navigate the complexities of human interaction and experience. Embracing this evolution without resistance curates a depth of maturity that, when coupled with the insights gleaned from God's Word, leads to true wisdom. The world needs more individuals who humbly walk in true wisdom and understand the importance of resilience in the face of challenges and complexities in the tapestry of life. Don't quit when life's challenges arise. Persist when the path grows steep. John Maxwell has said, "Everything worthwhile is uphill,"[55] which means that you must choose to keep walking even when things get hard; guided by your values, take one foot in front of the other, one step at a time, and grow and stretch yourself a little every day. You can't expect to climb uphill if you're stuck in downhill habits.

In difficult moments, remember the words of James:

---

[55] Maxwell, John C. *No Limits: Blow the CAP Off Your Capacity*. Hachette UK, 2017

"Count it all joy when you meet trials of various kinds, for you know that the testing of your faith produces steadfastness. And let steadfastness have its full effect, that you may be perfect and complete, lacking in nothing" (James 1:2-4).

Embrace both the good and the difficult times, for they refine your values and shape who you will become. Learn to walk with God and to trust Him more and more and cast all your care upon him, for He cares for you (1 Peter 5:6-7). Sometimes, this refining process may bring laughter, but more often, it will bring some tears. Yet, it is in these tears that the greatest values are forged, values that will sustain you through life's journey. The Psalmist declares that,

"The Lord has done great things for us. We are joyful. Those who sow in tears shall harvest with joyful shouting (Psalms 126:3, 5).

When faced with trials, it's natural to question their purpose and to seek ways to avoid or escape them. However, just as gold is refined by fire, so too are we refined by the trials we face. These trials, though difficult, have the potential to produce values such as endurance, character, and hope within us (Romans 5:3-5). They teach us patience, empathy, and resilience—values that are instrumental in navigating the challenges of life. So, rather than seeking to avoid trials, embrace them as opportunities for growth and transformation, knowing that God is with you in the middle of it all, using situations to mold you into the person He created you to be, guided by lasting values.

The Patience of God

I don't like how God seems to approach everything so patiently. Well, of course, I do like it—His patience is beautiful—but sometimes, it really annoys me. I want answers now. I don't want this to hurt. I don't want others to hurt. But life keeps happening; things change constantly, and God remains the same: steady, solid, unshaken. He's so patiently active that, at times, it almost feels unfair (but what do I know about fairness?). He allows the pain, the grief, the transitions, and the unknown. Yet He never overreacts. He doesn't fly off the handle like I do. He doesn't respond out of frustration. He just walks with us—patient, steady, unfazed—even through the darkest valleys. He's teaching us, preparing a table for us, forming us, and refusing to waste our sorrows. At times, it is deeply frustrating that God rarely gives direct answers, but, instead, He unfolds stories—slowly, methodically unfolding them in ways that force us to wait and trust. It feels risky for Him to do it that way, but He's not in a hurry.

We must learn—truly learn—what it means to trust Him in the waiting, to rest in the quiet certainty that His steady, unseen work is not only enough but exactly what we need. Even when our heart aches for resolution, for everything to be mended in an instant, He calls us to a deeper trust. And that? That is the real perspective shift.

This journey is anything but perfect. We will stumble, we will falter, and we will fail. But if we surrender—willingly, joyfully—to the hands of Jesus, if we allow Him to shape our vision through both the storms and the celebrations, then resilience will rise in us. And in that surrender, in that refining, we will find something unshakable: a hope no trial can steal, no darkness can dim, and no failure can undo.

Pause... Breathe... Reflect.

1. Are you waiting for life to be "perfect" before you can see the beauty in it?
2. What if the ashes in your life are the beginning of something sacred?
3. Can you allow the messiness of the journey to speak instead of silencing it in shame?

Word of God Speak

Isaiah 43:2

"When you pass through the waters, I will be with you, and when you pass through the rivers, they will not sweep over you. When you walk through the fire, you will not be burned; the flames will not set you ablaze."

Chapter 6
E – Engage With Teachability

I read a brilliant book by organizational psychologist, Professor Adam Grant called *Think Again*.[56] The book explores the concept of rethinking and encourages readers to embrace the power of changing their minds to foster personal and professional growth. The premise of the book is that in a rapidly changing world, being able to rethink one's convictions, opinions, habits, methods, and ideas is a crucial skill for growth and resilience. Grant argues that too often, people become entrenched in their existing opinions, leading to closed-mindedness, unteachableness, and an unwillingness to consider alternative viewpoints. This can hinder personal development, decision-making, and collaboration with others.

Throughout the book, Adam Grant presents various strategies and insights on how to cultivate a more open and flexible mindset. He delves into psychological principles and real-life examples to show the benefits of being willing to reassess and revise one's views based on new evidence or changing circumstances. Grant

---

[56] Grant, A. (2023). *Think Again: The Power of Knowing What You Don't Know*. Penguin.

emphasizes that rethinking is not a sign of weakness or flip-flopping but rather a sign of intellectual humility and teachability.

The difference between being entrenched and dislodged is the difference between stagnation and transformation. When you're entrenched, you've dug yourself into a comfortable, familiar trench—your opinions, frameworks, and routines become immovable. It feels safe, even if it's stifling. You become overly attached to ways of thinking or doing things, assuming they're unchangeable truths rather than temporary constructs. But dislodging is disruptive. It's uncomfortable, unsettling, and often feels like chaos at first. Yet, dislodging is exactly what leads to growth and resilience.

The year the tree fell on our house and our ministry fell apart was a painfully vivid season of being dislodged. It stripped me of false securities and pried me out of deeply ingrained patterns and beliefs that were never meant to remain permanent. By God's grace, I was able to remain teachable in the midst of it all, and what initially looked like destruction, God used as reconstruction. He dismantled what I had clung to so tightly—not to harm me, but to free me. It was in the dislodging that I began to see what needed to change, and slowly, the disorienting wilderness became a pathway to transformation. Entrenched, I was stuck. Dislodged, I began to move toward becoming the person God was always calling me to be. Teachability was the key.

Jesus constantly challenged the status quo, prompting people to rethink their beliefs. Jesus' teachings and actions disrupted religious and social norms, pushing people towards a new way of life based on His principles. When Jesus walked the earth, Judea was a cultural melting pot under Roman rule with significant Roman influences. The Jews, with their strict religious practices, revered the Torah and the Temple in Jerusalem. Jewish society was divided into various sects like the Pharisees and Sadducees,[57] each with their own interpretations of the law. The region also bore the mark of Hellenistic culture[58] from Alexander the Great's conquests, with Greek language and customs prevalent, especially in urban centers. Roman rule was strict, with heavy taxes and social inequalities. Jesus' revolutionary teachings offered a message of hope, love, and transformation that resonated deeply with people.

The cultural view of women was deeply patriarchal. Women were seen as inferior, with limited access to education and leadership. Yet, Jesus treated women with respect and dignity, engaging them as equals and elevating their significance. Temple worship was central to Jewish life. Temples were seen as the

---

[57] **Pharisees and Sadducees:** Two religious groups during Jesus's time with different beliefs and practices.
[58] **Hellenistic culture:** Greek-style culture and ideas that spread after Alexander the Great.

dwelling place of God's presence. However, Jesus challenged certain practices, emphasizing inner spirituality over external rituals. He also emphasized sacrificial love,[59] teaching people to love their neighbors and even their enemies, which was opposite to prevailing beliefs.

Jesus stressed the importance of inner purity and moral conduct over outward actions and championed humility and servant leadership. He broke social barriers, associated with outcasts, and redefined leadership as service. He challenged the strict observance of the Sabbath by performing healing acts and reinterpreting the Mosaic Law with a focus on love and compassion. He embraced and restored the worth of the marginalized, revealing God as a loving Father.

Jesus' interaction with the adulteress woman in John 8 caused many to rethink their convictions. He taught that life does not consist of material possessions but of relationships and eternal values. He welcomed sinners and outcasts, challenging social norms and helping people reset their priorities. Jesus' compassion extended to those suffering from physical ailments, breaking social stigmas. He taught non-retaliation, opposing the culture of revenge. Jesus fearlessly exposed hypocrisy among religious

---

[59] **Sacrificial love:** A kind of love that involves sacrificing one's own interest for the benefit of others.

leaders, challenging their outward righteousness while harboring impure motives.

In the Great Commandment, Jesus calls us to love Him with all our heart, mind, and strength. If our desires or affections are misdirected, He invites us to rediscover the beauty of His presence and truth. There is no growth without teachability.

The Power of Teachability

Isn't it annoying when you are trying to tell a friend about something new you've learned or experienced, and your friend rudely interrupts you and says, "Oh, I know that already!" Not only do you feel dejected, but there is no way of knowing if you had something new to impart to your friend. Remaining teachable while we go through life is of utmost importance because it's the only way to remain curious, learn, and grow spiritually, intellectually, emotionally, and even relationally. It helps us to connect with others and navigate life's complexities with humility, curiosity, dependency on the Holy Spirit, and continuous improvement that prevents us from becoming too resistant to change.

It is a valuable mindset that enhances every aspect of our lives and positively impacts those around us. It allows us to keep learning throughout our lives, which is essential in a rapidly changing world where new information and insights are constantly emerging. Many times, we assume that everyone interprets reality the way we do, and we seem puzzled and even frustrated when that is not the case. When we are open and willing to learn from others, expand our horizons, investigate our prejudices, question our intuitions, acknowledge our limitations and cultural imprints, and seek guidance, we become better equipped to overcome challenges and hear God's voice in the midst of it all. We are all born into specific cultural and situational circumstances, be it social, religious, political, or even economic. Sometimes, we expect the rest of the world to understand our context and worldview, and perhaps we even think less of them if they don't. Moreover, humility and openness help us differentiate between cultural and biblical convictions. That's a thought to toss into your mental mixer. Are you absolutely certain that your convictions are genuinely biblical, or could they just be a byproduct of the cultural soup you grew up in? It's a question worth digging into like a treasure hunt. You might uncover some surprising insights. But let's be real—this kind of soul-searching only works if you've got a teachable spirit. So, put on your explorer hat, keep an open mind, and get ready to embark on a journey of discovery!

Teachability requires humility, as it acknowledges that we do not have all the answers and that others can contribute to our understanding. It fosters self-awareness and helps us recognize areas where we can improve and grow. Being teachable enhances our ability to listen and empathize with others. When we are so convinced about our own point of view, we extremely rarely empathize or listen to others.

Teachability fosters constructive communication and collaboration, strengthening our relationships with family, friends, colleagues, and the broader community. It helps us remain open to new possibilities and ideas, making us more resilient and better equipped to navigate transitions. A teachable mindset encourages us to seek diverse perspectives when facing challenges. By considering various viewpoints and learning from the experiences of others, we can improve our problem-solving abilities. Teachability encourages us to explore new subjects, ask questions, and seek understanding, making life a continuous journey of discovery. Demonstrating teachability sets a positive example for others, inspiring them to embrace learning.

Teachability Breeds Growth

Remaining teachable as we walk with Jesus fosters spiritual growth, deepens our relationship with Him, and allows the Holy Spirit to guide and transform us (in every area) continually. It is a posture of humility and surrender that opens the door to an enriching and fulfilling journey with Christ. Remaining teachable is crucial for continuous spiritual growth because it acknowledges that there is always more to learn and understand about God, His beauty, grace, and His ways.

Somebody once said that change is the only constant in life. In some areas, change is non-existent. 1 + 1 will always be 2. Gravity will always pull us down, and when someone slaps you in the face, it hurts. However, as we go through life, we are confronted with massive internal and external changes. Thus, we need more continuing revelation and not so many closed systems of thinking.

We need to be okay with the unresolved along the way. Life is a journey, not a formula. We need to remain teachable and willing to rethink our convictions. I do believe absolutes absolutely exist, and sometimes we need black-and-white instructions (for children, for example). However, as we get older and once we've learned to look both ways before we cross the road, we are confronted with weightier things—things that require greater contemplation, teachability, nuance, humility, and observation rather than hasty judgment.

Sometimes, we build fortresses around our convictions because we want to protect ourselves or others. Many times, it is motivated by fear or past experiences or thinking that we are right and others are wrong. Often, when we are confronted with some unfiltered evil in this world, we want to shout from the rooftop, "THIS IS WRONG AND HERE IS WHY..." and rightfully so. Admittedly, at times, it is necessary to unwaveringly defend the conviction that if the person keeps walking towards the cliff, they will fall off and die. In some moments, immediate action is required rather than prolonged observation.

Nevertheless, are we even sure that it is a cliff the person is walking towards? Have we examined it thoroughly? Perhaps behind that rock is a diving board into a refreshing pool. A humble and teachable person allows the possibility that, sure, some things don't need to be questioned, but others need to be contemplated and potentially rethought. Wisdom allows us to see the difference between the two.

I don't have to rethink my decision to deny my 14-year-old daughter to go to the pool party of this 22-year-old jock from the neighborhood. However, I should never let my convictions stop me from empathetically listening to my kids about their thoughts and concerns even if, at the moment, I don't quite understand them or even disagree with them. In fact, in my own parenting journey, it's been my kids who have caused me to rethink many things.

Rookies

Teachability is a cornerstone of growth and resilience, and an often-overlooked aspect of teachability is recognizing that sometimes the best insights don't come from the experts but from the rookies. There's a certain freshness, a unique perspective that rookies bring to the table. Experts, while invaluable, can sometimes be trapped in their own experience, leading to blind spots.

In his other groundbreaking book *Hidden Potential*, Adam Grant draws a sharp contrast between experts and rookies—showing why, in certain moments, the fresh eyes of a rookie can be more valuable than the well-worn lens of an expert.[60]

These blind spots can prevent innovative thinking and new approaches. Interestingly, a leader's journey often involves balancing between what they see and what they fail to see. By engaging with rookies, leaders can tap into "rookie smarts" – the uninhibited curiosity, the willingness to question the status quo, and the drive to explore uncharted territories. Rookies haven't yet been conditioned to follow conventional wisdom, which means they might stumble upon creative solutions that an expert might overlook.

This doesn't diminish the value of expertise but rather complements it. By recognizing and utilizing the strengths of both the rookies and the experts, leaders can cultivate a dynamic environment where blind spots become opportunities for discovery rather than obstacles.

Therefore, in striving toward our goals, sometimes it's the

---

[60] Grant, A. (2023). *Hidden Potential: The Science of Achieving Greater Things*. Viking.

rookie's fresh eyes that can illuminate the path just as brightly as the expert's seasoned gaze. Embracing this duality ensures that we remain adaptable, innovative, and ultimately more successful.

John Maxwell, in his brilliant book *Thinking for a Change*, asks the question: "Is my desire for success and to improve my life strong enough to prompt me to change my thinking?"[61] Is my desire to walk in a deeper relationship with Jesus strong enough to prompt me to change my thinking? Is my desire to grow in empathy and to become a better husband, father, and leader strong enough to change my thinking? Is my desire to not miss the beauty in and around me strong enough to cause me to regularly investigate my worldview? Is my desire to contribute meaningfully to society and to see God's kingdom come on earth as it is in heaven strong enough to inspire me to rethink? Is my desire to be a part of the solution rather than the problem strong enough to move me to action once I have changed my thinking?

Let's Get Practical!

The Bible tells us that we have the power to direct or redirect our own thinking.

Finally, brothers, whatever is true, whatever is honorable, whatever is just, whatever is pure, whatever is lovely, whatever is

---

[61] Maxwell, J. C. (2003). *Thinking For A change: 11 Ways Highly Successful People Approach Life and Work*. Hachette UK.

commendable, if there is any excellence, if there is anything worthy of praise, think about these things. (Philippians 4:8)

When we're talking about rethinking, we're not talking about being *"tossed back and forth by the waves and blown here and there by every wind of teaching and by the cunning and craftiness of people in their deceitful scheming" (Eph 4:14).* We're not talking about being manipulated but about remaining malleable. Preventing ourselves from getting stuck in our ways of thinking requires intentional effort and a commitment to growth. Here are some practical steps we can all take:

1. Practice the fear of the Lord.

Years ago, I had an experience that forever reshaped my understanding of the fear of the Lord. We visited Niagara Falls, a place I had only seen in pictures and heard about in stories. As we walked alongside the river leading to the falls, I noticed how the water picked up speed, its roar growing louder with each step. The mist rose in the distance like a veil, hiding something both mysterious and powerful. Then, we turned the final corner—and there they were.

The sheer magnitude of the falls was overwhelming. The crashing water thundered in my ears, the mist soaked my skin, and for a moment, I was completely awestruck. Two emotions flooded me at once—ones that don't typically coexist. First, a childlike joy, an exhilaration that bubbled up from deep within, as if my soul itself was celebrating. But at the same time, a sobering awareness: this was no tame beauty. If I took one wrong step, if I lost my footing, the same breathtaking power that mesmerized me would consume me completely.

And that, I realized, is the fear of the Lord. God invites us to come to Him with childlike wonder, to delight in His presence— but we must never forget who we're dealing with. He is the Almighty, the Creator of heaven and earth, the One whose power commands both awe and reverence. Joy and holy fear—held together in perfect tension.

The biblical proverb that "the fear of the Lord is the beginning of wisdom" encapsulates the foundational principle that true wisdom stems from a reverential awe and respect for Yahweh and His word. This doesn't mean a fear of punishment. Instead, it emphasizes a deep desire to go after an understanding of God's character, motivations, love, and moral authority. When we recognize the greatness of God and humbly submit to His divine wisdom, we embark on a journey of seeking truth, integrity, and understanding. The fear of the Lord serves as the cornerstone of wisdom because it redirects human perspectives from self-centered desires toward aligning with God's purposes. By acknowledging God's supremacy and embracing His guidance, we open ourselves to His transformational wisdom that shapes our thoughts, choices, and relationships in ways that honors Jesus and leads to a life of purpose and meaning.

God is a generous God and gives wisdom when we ask Him (James 1:5).

Jesus' teachings offer timeless truths that are relevant across cultures and generations. His wisdom addresses fundamental human nature and the enduring challenges we face as a human race. When we truly walk through life with the fear of the Lord as our primary motivator, our eyes, minds, and hearts will be open to His leadership. It will prevent us from getting stuck in our own ways. So, we ought to read our bibles, pray, seek the Lord, and listen to His voice.

2. Cultivate Curiosity.

Sarah was a curious and inquisitive teenager who always had a thirst for knowledge. One day, at youth group, she noticed the pastor's wife outside, meticulously sketching the surrounding trees. Intrigued, she approached her and struck up a conversation. Mrs. Thompson explained that she had been an artist for many years and loved capturing the beauty of nature on paper. Over the next few weeks, Sarah and Mrs. Thompson would meet regularly. Sarah would watch as she sketched, and Mrs. Thompson would share stories of her artistic journey. Inspired by her passion, Sarah decided to try drawing herself. She borrowed some art supplies and began experimenting with different techniques. As Sarah practiced, she discovered a newfound love for art. She started observing the world around her more closely, noticing the play of light on leaves, the intricate details of flowers, and the subtle shades of color in the sky. Her curiosity led her to learn about various art styles, attend workshops, and read books on the subject. Years later, Sarah's curiosity had transformed her into a full-fledged talent. She pursued a degree in fine arts and became a successful artist known for her captivating landscapes. She often credited her encounter with Mrs. Thompson at youth group as the spark that ignited her curiosity and set her on a path of lifelong learning and creative exploration. Sarah's story serves as a reminder that asking questions, taking risks, and embracing curiosity can lead to unexpected passions and open doors to fulfilling and enriching experiences.

The German word for curiosity is *Neugier*. The word "Neugier" comes from Old High German and is composed of the words "niuwe" (new) and "giur" (desire). Therefore, it has an etymological connection to the idea of a desire or longing for something new, unknown, or interesting. Over time, the meaning of the word has evolved to describe the feeling or motivation to learn more about things that have been previously unknown or fascinating. Curiosity can serve as a driving force to expand knowledge and gain new experiences. We ought to approach life with a curious mindset. In order to foster curiosity, we need to continue to ask questions, listen, explore new topics, and seek to understand different perspectives. Embrace the joy of learning and discovering.

3. Read Widely.

Reading is important for numerous reasons, as it plays a vital role in our personal, spiritual, educational, and even societal development. Reading a wide array of books helps us to not get stuck in our ways. Reading is one of the primary ways to acquire new information, facts, ideas, and insights. It exposes us to a wide range of subjects, expanding our understanding of the world and fostering a lifelong pursuit of learning. Further, reading enhances language skills by exposing us to proper grammar, vocabulary, and sentence structures (most of the time!). It improves our ability to communicate effectively in both spoken and written forms. When I was learning English, reading books in English helped immensely. Engaging with written material stimulates cognitive functions such as critical thinking, analysis, problem-solving, and creativity. It exercises our brains and keeps our minds sharp.

My wife loves to read fiction, and she argues that fiction and imaginative literature encourage the development of creativity and imagination. It transports us to different worlds, cultures, and time, allowing us to envision scenarios beyond our immediate reality. Reading ought to expose us to diverse perspectives, cultures, and characters, fostering empathy and understanding. It helps us see the world through others' eyes and builds our capacity for compassion. Reading is a fundamental skill for academic success. It is essential for understanding course materials, completing assignments, and performing well on exams. Reading can even be a form of relaxation and stress reduction.

"Wer liest, der lernt; und wer lernt, der leitet." When my kids were younger, I would often tell them, "Those who read will learn, and those who learn will lead." It was one of those phrases that sounded wise at the time. Honestly, I still believe in the power of reading—though, as a young boy, I wasn't exactly devouring novels or philosophical tomes myself. My dad tried to get me to read books when I was a teenager with little prevail. It wasn't until my late teens and early twenties that I discovered the power of reading. I began to engage with books and other resources that cover a wide range of subjects, viewpoints, and cultures. This helped broaden my understanding tremendously and deepened my relationship with God and others greatly.

If I could revise that phrase now, I'd say, "Those who read and learn will lead." Plenty of people can read words on a page, but not everyone internalizes what they read. Comprehension and application are worlds apart. The same goes for listening. Many hear words, but few truly listen to the heart behind them. Real, transformative learning isn't about how many books you've read or how many podcasts you've listened to; it's about how deeply those truths have marked you. Ink on a page means nothing if it doesn't become ink on the heart. Leadership isn't born from an accumulation of knowledge but from the kind of understanding that changes how you live and think.

4. Listen Actively.

Many years ago, I read a book called The 7 Habits of Highly Effective People by Stephen Covey. This book is considered a classic and essential for good reasons. All 7 habits in this book can transform our thinking. Particularly, habit 5 changed my life: "Seek First to Understand, Then to Be Understood."[62] This habit underscores the importance of empathetic and effective communication. Covey emphasizes that true communication involves genuinely listening to others with the intent to understand their perspectives, feelings, and needs before expressing our own ideas or opinions. By taking the time to empathetically listen, we create an environment of trust and respect, which paves the way for more productive and meaningful interactions. Habit 5

---

[62] Covey, S. R. (2004). *The 7 Habits of Highly Effective People: Powerful Lessons in Personal Change.* Simon and Schuster.

encourages us to step outside our own frame of reference and seek a deeper understanding of others' viewpoints, allowing for more collaborative problem-solving and fostering stronger connections in both personal and professional relationships. To not get stuck in our ways, we need to practice active listening when engaging in conversations. We ought to give others our full attention, ask follow-up questions, and genuinely try to understand their point of view.

5. *Travel and Exposure.*

As a missionary, my life has been a passport stamped with unforgettable moments and profound lessons. I've sipped sweet chai on the dusty side roads of Pakistan and relished the fiery spices of Korean cuisine alongside the vibrant zest of Brazilian passion. I've marveled at the majesty of the pyramids in Egypt from the back of a camel and shared the Gospel in the hidden corners of Eastern Europe. I've walked among the ancient ruins of Greece and Scotland, their stories etched into time and prayed with refugees whose resilience shines brighter than their hardships. I've braved the icy chills of Canada and Sweden, sung worship songs barefoot on Australian beaches, hiked the breathtaking Alps in Italy and Austria, and ascended the Eiffel Tower to gaze upon the City of Light.

These journeys have been about God's kingdom and His

people—the countless faces, cultures, and stories have shaped me. For over two decades, I've seen young lives transformed by stepping out of their comfort zones and into the unknown. Teachability blooms when we're willing to be confronted by the unfamiliar, allowing it to reshape us. Every culture, no matter how foreign, carries its unique beauty—a reflection of God's creativity.

So here's my advice: don't pour all your resources into accumulating stuff that gathers dust. Invest in travel. Let the world teach you, awe you and stretch you. Immerse yourself in the breathtaking diversity of God's creation, and you'll return richer in spirit, humility, and perspective than you ever imagined.

6. *Engage in Discussions, Seek Feedback, and Regularly Reflect and Self-Assess.*

We should participate in open and respectful discussions with people who hold different opinions. Engaging in healthy debates can expose us to new ideas and help us refine our own perspectives. We can and should welcome constructive feedback from friends, family, colleagues, and, at times, even from those with whom we disagree. Constructive criticism can help us identify blind spots and areas where our thinking might be limited. Regular reflection on our thoughts, values, and opinions is invaluable. Prayerful self-assessment helps us identify areas for improvement.

7. *Stay Humble.*

Even in learning and rethinking, we need to remain humble. When we get a new revelation or learn a new insight, some of us immediately want to turn around and teach others our newfound wisdom. However, new revelations and new insights, most of the time, need a gestation period to develop and take root in our own hearts and minds first before we can even consider passing them on. Sometimes, we're too quick and arrogant to think that everybody needs to hear what we've just learned. Many times, God trusts us with a piece or a nugget of revelation to see if we, in turn, trust Him to reveal more of it in due time. If we conceitedly share an unfinished picture, we're not doing ourselves or the recipient any favor. We always have to acknowledge that no one has all the answers and continue to cultivate humility.

8. *Practice Mindfulness and Take Breaks from Technology.*

Mindfulness helps us stay present and open to our thoughts and feelings. It can also help us become aware of any rigid thought patterns we might have. To meditate is a biblical concept, and we ought to slow down our breathing and become more aware of God, ourselves, and our surroundings regularly. Disconnecting from the constant streams of information and social media is indispensable for a healthy mind. This can give us the needed mental space to reflect and think critically. Slowing down your breathing, practicing meditation, and cultivating mindfulness offers a wide range of physical, mental, spiritual, and emotional benefits. In Eastern religions, meditation insists that we empty our minds. Biblical meditation exhorts us to fill our minds and hearts with Jesus.

"I will ponder all your work and meditate on your mighty deeds"
(Psalm 77:12).

Frequently, we ought to disconnect from all screens, take time to ponder, give our brains more oxygen, lower our blood pressure, increase our God and self-awareness, connect our hearts to Jesus, and strengthen ourselves in the Lord (1 Samuel 30:6).

9. *Challenge Confirmation Bias[63] and Regularly Reevaluate Convictions.*

We need to be aware of our tendency to seek out information that confirms our existing beliefs. We ought to make an effort to seek out differing viewpoints. We should set aside time to reevaluate our values and convictions periodically. As we gain new insights, we should be willing to adjust our habits, values, methods, and convictions accordingly. Again, the Bible encourages us to live a life of constant renewal of our minds. The Holy Spirit loves to help us navigate through the daily onslaught of data and

---

[63] **Confirmation bias:** Only paying attention to things that agree with what you already believe.

lead us to the truth.

"The Lord is my shepherd; I shall not want. He makes me lie down in green pastures. He leads me beside still waters. He restores my soul. He leads me in paths of righteousness for His name's sake" (Psalm 23:1-2 ESV).

Life's journey is every so often marked by a bittersweet reality: we come to wisdom just as our physical vitality begins to wane. This paradoxical truth highlights the importance of seeking wisdom, remaining teachable, and living purposefully at every stage of life. In Ecclesiastes 12:1, we are reminded to

"Remember your Creator in the days of your youth, before the days of trouble come."

This verse emphasizes the importance of seeking wisdom and living intentionally from a young age. Similarly, Proverbs 16:31 states,

"Gray hair is a crown of splendor; it is attained in the way of righteousness."

This verse encourages us to view aging as a process that brings its own unique beauty and wisdom.

As we wrap up this chapter, let's take a moment to appreciate the superhero duo of humility and teachability. They're like

Batman and Robin for our soul—always ready to save the day, as long as we're willing to suit up with a little curiosity. Stay open to new ideas, experiences, and perspectives—because, spoiler alert, nobody ever grew wiser by saying, "I know it all already." Dive into activities that make your brain do cartwheels, like learning a new skill, picking up a quirky hobby, or finally figuring out how to use a Nintendo Switch (bonus points if you ask a teenager to help).

Build bridges with people of all ages. Young folks keep you in the loop with fresh ideas (and confusing slang), while older generations hand you a treasure map of wisdom—if you're smart enough to listen. Take care of your body like it's the only one you've got (because it is). Regular exercise, a healthy diet, and good sleep aren't just nice ideas—they're your backstage pass to a life that doesn't groan every time it stands up.

And let's not forget your mind and spirit. Pray, meditate, and spend time with the Lord daily. Let His Word shape your thoughts, go to church even when brunch is tempting, and, if needed, see a counselor to help sort out life's messiness. Keep a journal—because one day, your grandkids will love to read about how you conquered life's curveballs (and also because writing things down makes you feel fancy).

Remain teachable! Life is like an ever-changing dance floor. The music shifts, and sometimes the steps get tricky, but Jesus is always there to lead. So, embrace the changes, take the lessons, laugh at the missteps, and trust that you're never dancing alone.

Pause... Breathe... Reflect.

1. Are you more committed to being right or being refined?
2. What is God trying to teach you right now through discomfort or disagreement?
3. Who or what has challenged your thinking lately—and how did you respond?

Word of God Speak

Proverbs 1:5

"Let the wise hear and increase in learning, and the one who understands obtain guidance."

Chapter 7
C – Choose Rest

I learned about the connection between rest and resilience through a very difficult experience. It all began with a brief conversation between my pastor and me back in October 2023. I had been wrestling with different emotions of defeat, grief, frustration, and visionlessness[64] in life and ministry. Since September of 2022, our campus had been going through a tremendously difficult transitional time, which, at one point, caused me to pack up my office and, at least emotionally, leave. I was ready to leave behind 22 years of investment, laughter, tears, deep frustrations, and amazing times in the presence of Jesus and the nations of the world. However, things didn't turn out the way everyone had thought. I was asked if I could imagine being a part of rebuilding the ministry. It was emotionally taxing, to say the least.

Now, with all that weight on my heart, I said to my pastor after he asked me how I was doing: "Well, I've been wrestling with some things!" Brevity was my pastor's calling card. So, all he said

---

[64] **Visionlessness:** A lack of direction, purpose, or motivation in life or ministry.

in reply was: "You can stop. God's going to win anyway!" I politely thanked him for that brief and, to be honest, hard-to-comprehend comment and walked back to my office. When I sat down in my chair, I began to pray, inquiring of the Lord how that would be possible. How do I stop wrestling and calm the internal turmoil I was sensing?

Out of the blue, my dad's face appeared in my mind's eyes. I hadn't thought about him lately, but here he was, gentle, smiling, approachable, loving. It was as if the Father in heaven spoke directly to my wounded and weary heart: "You don't have to wrestle anymore. You just need a hug!"

Subsequently, for the next hour or so, I sat at my desk, drenched in tears, overwhelmed by the sheer reality of that moment. I needed a hug. I needed an embrace of eternity, a hug from the Father. I needed my reserves[65] replenished. I had neglected to come to the place of refuge in God for a long time. Perhaps I had visited from time to time but not dwelled there. I thought I got things under control. I thought I was the savior of it all.

The Bible tells us to not grow weary in doing good. But what do you do when doing good becomes a challenge because you

---

[65] **Reserves:** The inner capacity (mental and emotional energy) to cope with stress and responsibilities.

have grown so weary?

I realized that over the last several years, I had overexerted my emotional, spiritual, and probably cognitive resources. Such depletion can, at least in part, be a cause for loss of motivation. I had been wrestling with myself, trying to maintain control in every area (ministry, parenting, marriage, fundraising), partly maintaining an image of myself in front of others that was not quite true, and carrying the weight of internal dissonance.[66] At the same time, I was neglecting rest and spending time with Jesus. We can spend our lives chasing self-actualization, defining ourselves by others' opinions or an idealized version of who we think we should be. But true freedom isn't found in obsessing over ourselves—it's found in beholding the beauty of Jesus. When we fix our eyes on Him, He shapes our identity and fulfills the deepest desires of our hearts.

In her tremendously helpful book, *Invitation to Retreat*, Ruth Haley Barton confesses that "it is that constant trying so hard on so many fronts all the time that often leaves me on the brink of exhaustion."[67] Back in October 2023, I had reached a critical point of exhaustion and discouragement, which caused a lack of

---

[66] **Internal dissonance:** Psychological tension caused by conflicting beliefs, behaviors, or values.
[67] Barton, Ruth Haley. *Invitation to Retreat: The Gift and Necessity of Time Away with God*. InterVarsity Press, 2018.

motivation and clarity of vision. My reserves were depleted. Nobel Prize winner Daniel Kahneman notes: "If you have had to force yourself to do something, you are less willing or less able to exert self-control when the next challenge comes around."[68] In other words, if you constantly use your own strength and even tap into the deepest reservoirs without refilling them, you will run out of energy and motivation. If you've had to compel yourself to take action, your willingness and capacity to exercise self-control, gain new perspectives, and be empathetic toward others will eventually diminish.

For a long time, I forced myself to pretend I was stronger than I actually was. I forced myself to overlook the reality that frustration and anger are not the right tools to get anything accomplished (James 1:20). I fooled myself into thinking that an entitled attitude of "I deserve this" can lead to rest and recuperation (hence, I ate and drank too much). Even though sometimes, after a long day of meetings, I'm depleted and exhausted, it is not okay to turn into a non-thinking zombie.

I had developed a belief that I could control outcomes, narratives, and even people. Sometimes, I got disproportionately frustrated with people whose lack of preparation or skill made more work for me or others—at times rightfully so, but still

---

[68] Kahneman, Daniel. *Thinking, Fast and Slow*. Penguin UK, 2011.

disproportionally. I had forced myself for years to not take inventory of my emotional state. I had become cynical[69] and critical, perhaps even dismissive toward people, their stories, and their expressions. In many areas of my life over the years, I had forced myself to chase after concocted ideals rather than living in reality and truly longing to see God's dreams and purposes come forth.

I put too much confidence in myself, wanting to be the one in charge and the one who gets the credit. I became frustrated by my perceived and real limitations and tried to avoid acknowledging them. I didn't want people telling me what to do, so I pretended to be knowledgeable and experienced, even when I wasn't. I had compelled myself to live under the self-made and unhealthy pressure of FOMO,[70] the urge to fix things and solve problems, and trying to be my own and other people's savior. It ultimately eroded my trust in God. For me, FOMO was not just the fear of missing out but also the fear of not getting it done, the fear of lack, the fear of not being provided for, the fear of not being good enough, the fear of getting lost, the fear of not being recognized, the fear of regret. This kind of fear empties your reserves quickly.

---

[69] **Cynicism:** A skeptical or negative attitude that often stems from emotional exhaustion or disappointment
[70] **FOMO (Fear of Missing Out):** Worrying that you're missing something fun or important.

Because I was empty, emotionally and spiritually, I lacked both the willingness and the ability to exert self-control, to have a sober mind, to apply energy to do good and serve others, and to remain motivated. Love had grown a bit cold in my heart. Sure, such mental, spiritual, emotional, and cognitive depletion can be alleviated by some simple, practical steps, such as a better diet (increased glucose intake), improved sleep, regular meditation, exercise, etc. But there was more. A more profound longing for shalom and resilience was needed. I wanted to become aware of when my heart burned with resonance and when it burned with resistance.

In October of 2023, I found myself at emotional rock bottom. I reached out to my leaders, and they graciously allowed me to take a short sabbatical. I needed rest! After nearly two months of focusing on and intentionally disconnecting from the busyness of life, I found myself rediscovering the profound significance of rest and the rejuvenating presence of Jesus. It's no coincidence that the commandment to keep the Sabbath holy is placed next to the commandment against murder. Neglecting regular Sabbath rest can be a form of self-harm, a slow erosion of our well-being. Resilience isn't just forged in the crucible of hardship; it's also nurtured through regular and intentional retreat and rest.

During my time of unplugging, I realized that rest isn't just about physical rejuvenation; it's about spiritual and emotional replenishment. In Matthew 11:28-29, Jesus says,

"Come (initiative) to me (location), all you who are weary and burdened (vulnerability), and I will give you rest. Take my yoke upon you (engagement) and learn from me (teachability), for I am gentle and humble in heart, and you will find rest for your souls."

True rest, as Jesus invites us to experience in Matthew 11:28-29, requires more than just stepping back from work. It involves active qualities—initiative, vulnerability, teachability, engagement, and a spiritual shift in perspective—each of which transforms our approach to rest on a soul-deep level and fills our resilience reservoir.

First, initiative is crucial; we must choose to seek rest purposefully, as Jesus calls us to "come" to Him. This act of coming to Jesus is a deliberate decision to prioritize rest and connect with Him, setting aside time and space, even when it feels like one more thing on the to-do list.

Next, true rest involves vulnerability. Jesus' invitation is for "all you who are weary and burdened." He isn't asking us to show up perfect or self-sufficient; He's asking us to bring our weariness and burdens openly. A practical application of vulnerability is expressing your struggles to God in prayer, admitting when you're feeling overwhelmed, or even sharing your challenges with a trusted friend who can pray with you. Vulnerability opens the door to genuine healing and rest because it requires us to admit our limitations, creating space for God to work.

Teachability is another essential element, as we have already discovered in previous chapters. Jesus tells us to "learn" from Him, reminding us that real rest isn't simply disengaging but being open to new ways of living and thinking. When we're teachable, we recognize that perhaps our current ways aren't serving us well and that there might be a better way forward.

Then there's engagement—"Take my yoke[71] upon you." A yoke requires two to move together, and this partnership implies that rest isn't merely inactivity but a shared effort with Christ. Engagement means actively involving God in every part of life, inviting Him to carry the load with us. Practically, this can mean taking intentional breaks throughout the day to breathe, pray, or refocus on Jesus, recognizing that rest isn't about completely disengaging but about being present with God.

Finally, rest requires a spiritual change of location. Jesus says, "Come to me," emphasizing that true rest is found when we're near Him. This could mean prioritizing time in worship, prayer, or a peaceful walk to reconnect with God. This "change of location"

---

[71] **Yoke:** A wooden bar used to connect animals. Jesus used it to talk about learning and working closely with Him.

doesn't necessarily have to be physical, although that can be helpful. It is a movement of the heart and mind toward Christ. It's a reminder that in the noise of life, rest is not simply ceasing activity but drawing close to God in trust, even in the middle of daily demands. When we embrace these five elements of rest—initiative, vulnerability, teachability, engagement, and a spiritual change of location—we find that God's rest sustains us, refuels us, and restores us far more deeply than any amount of worldly downtime ever could.

He Makes Me Lie Down

Alex Soojung-Kim Pang writes: "You have to resist the lure of busyness, make time for rest, take it seriously, and protect it from a world that is intent on stealing it."[72]

As I experienced back in October of 2023, neglecting timely rest is akin to playing a dangerous game with emotional burnout. It's like trying to sprint a marathon; you might push hard for a while, but eventually, you'll hit a wall. Emotional burnout isn't just a temporary setback; it's a draining, relentless condition that saps your energy, dampens your enthusiasm, and dulls your focus. It's a slow erosion of your cognitive abilities, leaving you feeling depleted and disconnected.

---

[72] Pang, Alex Soojung-Kim. *Rest: Why You Get More Done When You Work Less.* Penguin UK, 2016.

In our fast-paced, achievement-oriented culture, we often overlook the importance of rest and retreat. We glorify busyness and productivity, applaud the person who works 18 hours a day all year long, and equate hustle and bustle with success and value. However, true resilience and effectiveness are found in the rhythm of work and rest, in the balance of activity and stillness. Work diligently and intentionally, but guard your rest with equal fervor. As Psalm 23:2-3 says,

"He makes me lie down in green pastures, He leads me beside quiet waters, He refreshes my soul. He guides me along the right paths for His name's sake."

God invites us to find rest and refreshment in focusing on Him, to trust in His provision and care even amid life's challenges. That is the place where we can sing a chorus during chaos.

Solitude and Retreat

Ruth Haley Barton writes, "By relinquishing normal patterns of human striving and hard work, we can become aware of the vacuum we keep trying to fill by doing stuff and achieving things...In the stillness of retreat, I can see more clearly how I am being pushed and pulled by other people's expectations, by my own inner compulsions, and by the basic necessities of life in our culture, and I realize how far I've drifted from living my heart's truest desire."[73]

Solitude and retreat not only refill our reserves but have a profound impact in revealing the underlying motivations and desires that drive our lives. In the busyness of life, we often fill our time with activities and achievements, seeking to fulfill a deep-seated need within us. However, true fulfillment cannot be found solely in external accomplishments. The Bible provides insights into the importance of solitude and reflection. In Psalm 46:10, we are urged to

"Be still, and know that I am God."

It is indispensable to regularly quiet our minds and hearts to recognize God's presence and guidance in our lives. Similarly, in Mark 6:31, Jesus invites His disciples to

"Come with me by yourselves to a quiet place and get some rest."

This demonstrates Jesus' recognition of the need for solitude and rest amidst the demands of ministry. We can incorporate periods of solitude and retreat into our lives to reconnect with our deepest desires and refocus our priorities. This can involve setting aside time each day for quiet reflection, engaging in activities that bring us peace and joy, and filling our tanks, as well as seeking

---

[73] Barton, Ruth Haley. *Invitation to Retreat: The Gift and Necessity of Time Away with God.* InterVarsity Press, 2018.

guidance through prayer and meditation. By relinquishing the constant striving and busyness, we replenish our reserves. We also create space to listen to the beautifully encouraging voice of our Father in heaven, and it will realign our lives with His purposes.

Resilience is not a fixed trait but a set of behaviors, thoughts, and actions that can be learned and developed. In his book *Resilient*, John Eldredge writes: "Human beings are at the same time resilient and unpredictably fragile."[74] John goes on to assert that humans are incredibly resilient and capable of remarkable feats driven by a primal instinct for survival. We see examples like Saint John turning suffering into beauty and Nelson Mandela forgiving after enduring years in prison. Yet, this resilience can suddenly vanish. Sometimes, after years of giving, a person might make a drastic change, like a mother having an affair or a minister losing faith. It is often a result of emotional burnout. We can endure hardship for years, but eventually, our hearts may give out, and we give up the fight. We can see this everywhere as people struggle with depleted reserves. While we can rally and have done so, each rally further depletes our reserves. This is the trauma cycle: we endure harm, deny it, seek solace, and often respond with rage when our efforts are blocked. Our reserves reinforce our

---

[74] Eldredge, John. Resilient: *Restoring Your Weary Soul in These Turbulent Times*. Thomas Nelson, 2022.

resilience. Rest reinforces our reserves.

No Rest Without a Shepherd

Our focus on Jesus is paramount in this journey of resilience. In his foreword to Robert Morris' book *Take The Day Off*, Max Lucado writes: "For sheep to sleep, everything must be just right. No predators. No tension in the flock. No bugs in the air. No hunger in the belly. Everything has to be just so. Unfortunately, the sheep cannot find safe pasture, nor can they spray insecticide, deal with the frictions, or find food. They need help. They need a shepherd to help them lie down in green pastures. Without a shepherd, they can't rest. Without a shepherd, neither can we."[75]

Jesus, our Good Shepherd, tenderly cares for us, guiding us away from the perilous cliffs of despair and into the lush pastures of hope and restoration. His heart beats with compassion, longing to see us thrive in the abundance of life He offers. We don't need to work for Him, but He invites us to work with Him. We want to bear fruit, not as over-compensation for our insecurities but to glorify the Father. In His presence, our fears are disarmed, and our strength is renewed. He beckons us to the banquet He has prepared, where He sits as the host, eager to commune with us and nourish our souls. At this table, we find not only physical

---

[75] Morris, Robert. *Take the Day Off: Receiving God's Gift of Rest*. FaithWords, 2019.

sustenance but also the spiritual nourishment that fuels our resilience.

Here, in the company of our Lord and Savior, we are fortified for the journey ahead. Jesus' desire for us is not a life free of challenges but a life empowered to overcome them. He walks with us through the valleys of adversity, offering His strength as we grow our spiritual muscles and navigate the rugged terrain. His promise is not that we will never face hardships but that in Him, we will find the resilience to rise above them.

So, Rest Well!

Many people are waking up to the importance of building rhythms of rest into their lives, and that's fantastic! But here's the thing—if you're resting in the "wrong" way, it may not actually be as beneficial as it could be. Rest isn't one-size-fits-all. You have to identify how you're weary before you can rest effectively. Think of it like a prescription: if you've got a headache, you don't treat it by putting a bandage on your knee. Likewise, if your exhaustion is physical, mental, emotional, or even spiritual, your rest needs to match the need. Let's break it down, shall we?

Physically tired? Look, sometimes you just need to embrace the nap. Schedule consistent sleep—none of that "I'll sleep when I'm dead" nonsense. Hydrate well (coffee and water, people), hug a loved one (because oxytocin is real), and move your body.

175

Exercise and stretching not only help alleviate physical fatigue but also release tension. Breathing exercises and even a good, deep belly laugh can work wonders. Oh, and eat something that fuels you—maybe not that third donut, though.

Mentally tired? When your brain feels like a tangled ball of yarn, it's time to unwind—literally. Laugh, get outside, and soak up some nature. Listen to music or create something, whether it's a painting, a new recipe, or even just a color-coded list. Take a break from the constant input of media (yes, that includes doom-scrolling), and communicate meaningfully—write a thank-you card or call a friend. You'll be amazed how much clarity comes from stepping back.

Emotionally tired? Emotional exhaustion can feel like you're carrying the weight of the world, so lighten the load. Start with gratitude, and make a list of things you're thankful for. Journal your thoughts and feelings, even if it's messy and raw. Celebrate something small, even if it's just making it through the day. Find some solitude and clarify expectations in your relationships. Most importantly, identify unhealthy patterns and take steps to address them. Emotional rest is about unburdening your heart.

Spiritually tired? When your soul feels parched, lean into God's Word. Worship and meditate on scripture or explore a new translation of the Bible to bring fresh insight. Establish consistent

Sabbaths (God knew what He was doing with that command), and deal with lingering conflict that's weighing you down. Spiritual rest is about reconnecting with God's peace and realigning with His purpose.

Sensory overload? This one's sneaky—sometimes it's not just your mind or heart that's fried but your senses. Step away from screens, avoid loud environments, and take a quiet walk. Even a nap can help reset your sensory system. Think of it as hitting the "mute" button on the chaos around you.

Socially tired? Not every invitation deserves a "yes." If you're drained from social interactions, give yourself permission to say no to things that deplete you. Instead, lean into life-giving relationships and situations that refresh your soul. Balance social rest with alone time, doing what you love most—whether that's reading, gardening, or just sitting with your thoughts.

Creatively tired? Feeling uninspired? Shake things up! If you usually draw, try songwriting. If you paint, maybe give an instrument a whirl. Creativity thrives on novelty, so experimenting with something new can recharge your creative energy.

Ultimately, rest is about being intentional and finding what truly renews you in every area of life. When you rest well, you're not just restoring yourself—you're equipping yourself to better reflect Jesus in your relationships, your work, and your ministry.

Explore new ways of resting, and watch how it transforms your ability to share His love with others.

Pause… Breathe… Reflect.

1. What does your pace of life say about what you believe is sustaining you?
2. Where are you hustling out of fear instead of resting in trust?
3. Do you view rest as weakness or worship? Why might that need to change?

Word of God Speak

Matthew 11:28-29

"Come to me, all you who are weary and burdened, and I will give you rest…"

Chapter 8
T – Trusting the Turns

I went to the store for what was supposed to be a quick in-and-out mission. Just a couple of items, nothing complicated. I grabbed what I needed, made my way to the self-checkout line, and breezed through the scan-and-bag. Then came time to pay. I pulled out a $20 bill, fed it to the machine, and… chaos. The machine blinked red, and a loud alarm blared, drawing more attention than a Walmart sale on Black Friday. My $20 bill had jammed in the machine, ripping in two, and I was officially that guy holding up the line.

Instantly, a crew of employees appeared, armed with keys and determination to rescue my mangled $20. My first reaction was to label this a complete disaster. I could feel irritation bubbling up—my plan for the day interrupted, my cash in shreds. But then, I remembered something: I actually didn't know if this was a "bad" thing or not. What if I just let this happen without judgment? So, I took a deep breath, let go of the frustration, and watched it unfold.

And it changed everything. As I let go, my heartbeat slowed, the irritation dissolved, and, strangely enough, I found myself genuinely appreciating the store employees who were doing their best to fix the machine and retrieve my money. After a few minutes, they handed me a fresh $20 bill. I paid with my card instead and walked out, no worse for wear. I hadn't burned any bridges, and I wasn't carrying a cloud of anger with me for the rest of the day.

In the end, letting go of my first reaction saved me a ton of frustration. It taught me that resilience grows when we refuse to let a setback define our mood or our day. It's a reminder: the first reaction may feel powerful, but it's the second response—the one where we decide not to judge the event—that actually builds strength.

As humans, we have an almost instinctive need to label events in our lives as either good or bad. It gives us a sense of control, a feeling of clarity in a world that is often anything but clear. However, this rush to judgment can prevent us from fully appreciating the complexities and long-term effects of what we experience. The ancient Chinese fable of the farmer and his horse captures this dynamic beautifully, offering profound wisdom about the nature of life and our often misguided reactions to it.

The story begins with a farmer who has only one horse. One day, the horse runs away, leaving the farmer without his primary means of labor and transportation. The neighbors rush to console him, declaring, "What terrible misfortune!" The farmer, calm and composed, responds, "Maybe." The next day, the horse returns, bringing with it a wild stallion. The neighbors, now jubilant, exclaim, "What wonderful fortune!" Again, the farmer replies, "Maybe."

The story doesn't stop there. The farmer's son tries to tame the wild stallion, but in the process, he is thrown off and breaks his leg. The neighbors, as predictable as ever, mourn with the farmer, saying, "What bad luck!" The farmer, steady as a rock, answers once more, "Maybe." Not long after, soldiers come to the village to conscript young men for a distant and dangerous war. Because of his broken leg, the farmer's son is spared. The neighbors, marveling at this unexpected turn, proclaim, "What incredible luck!" And the farmer, wise as ever, responds with his characteristic, "Maybe."

This fable is a powerful reminder of how shortsighted our judgments can be. What appears to be a disaster today might pave the way for something wonderful tomorrow. Life is rarely as simple as we try to make it with our quick labels of "good" or "bad." It is layered, complex, and often unresolved, and our perspective on events shifts as time and experience unfold the bigger picture.

Too often, we fail to account for the unknown and the unseen. We label something as "bad" simply because it brings discomfort, pain, or loss. Yet some of life's most painful moments carry the seeds of our greatest growth. Losing a job, for example, can feel devastating, but it might lead to a new opportunity that aligns more closely with your passions or gifts. A season of heartbreak might feel unbearable, but it could also become a period of profound self-discovery and healing, even bringing you closer to God.

On the other hand, not everything that feels "good" in the moment is truly beneficial. A glamorous promotion might come with stress that strains your relationships or compromises your health. That thrilling new opportunity might pull you away from your purpose.

Living in the unresolved requires humility, faith, and patience. It challenges us to embrace the mystery of life rather than rushing to conclusions. The fable of the farmer reminds us that we often lack the perspective to see the full picture. What's most important is not whether an event feels good or bad in the moment but how we respond and what we learn from it.

Instead of labeling every event, we can practice gratitude for the journey itself, knowing that God sees the entire story even when we cannot. Whether it's a "good" moment or a "bad" one—or something that defies simple categorization—let us trust that the ultimate narrative is being written by the One who knows the end from the beginning. Let us hold loosely to our judgments and tightly to our faith, allowing the unresolved to shape us in ways we might not yet understand.

Tactical Patience

Tactical patience is the disciplined art of giving a situation enough space to breathe, unfold, and reveal its true nature before rushing to assign meaning or act on it. It's about resisting the reflex to label every event as "good" or "bad" in the heat of the moment, which so often leads to premature reactions that complicate things further. Tactical patience isn't passivity; it's strategic restraint, a conscious decision to delay judgment until you have the full picture.

Sometimes, it's as brief as pausing for a few seconds to take a deep breath and recalibrate. Other times, it means waiting for hours or days to let emotions settle and clarity emerge. In rare cases, it might take months or even years to understand the deeper significance of what you're experiencing. This kind of patience builds resilience because it creates a buffer between stimulus and response, reducing the likelihood of impulsive overreactions. It transforms you from a reactive responder into a thoughtful observer, capable of engaging with situations from a place of wisdom and strength rather than fear or frustration. Tactical patience is not just waiting—it's waiting with intention, trusting that time will offer insight you wouldn't have seen in the rush to react. Trust the turns!

Steps to Practicing Tactical Patience and Trusting the Turns

1. Pause and Breathe Before Reacting.

Yes, here again with the breathing. It is that important. When something unexpected happens, our instinct is to immediately assign meaning—either as a blessing or a disaster. But Proverbs 18:13 warns,

"To answer before listening—that is folly and shame."

Instead of reacting impulsively, take a moment to breathe. Count to ten if needed. Let your emotions settle before engaging with the situation. Tactical patience begins with slowing down.

2. Acknowledge That You Don't Have All the Information.

We often assume we understand a situation when, in reality, we see only a fraction of the whole picture. Before deciding whether something is good or bad, remind yourself: I don't know everything yet. Time has a way of revealing things we couldn't see in the moment.

3. Pray for Perspective, Not Just Answers.

Instead of asking, 'Why is this happening?' ask the Lord, 'How do You want me to see this?' James 1:5 encourages us to seek wisdom from God, who gives generously. Prayer shifts our focus from frantic problem-solving to trusting that God is working in ways we can't yet understand.

4. Resist the Urge to Make Permanent Judgments on Temporary Situations.

Joseph's story in Genesis 37–50 is a perfect example. Sold into slavery, falsely accused, and thrown into prison, he could have easily labeled his life as cursed. But years later, he told his brothers, in Gen 50:20,

> *"You intended to harm me, but God intended it for good."*

What looks like a disaster today may be the setup for a miracle tomorrow.

5. Let Time Be a Filter.

Time has a way of sifting truth from emotion. What seems unbearable now may feel different in a week, a month, or a year. Tactical patience means resisting snap decisions and allowing God's timing to reveal what's true. Ecclesiastes 3:1 reminds us,

> *"There is a time for everything and a season for every activity under the heavens."*

6. Practice Gratitude, Even in Uncertainty.

When faced with a situation you don't understand, look for what you can be grateful for. 1 Thessalonians 5:18 says,

"Give thanks in all circumstances, for this is God's will for you in Christ Jesus."

Gratitude shifts your focus from fear and frustration to trust and expectation.

7. Seek Wise Counsel Before Drawing Conclusions.

Proverbs 11:14 tells us,

"Where there is no guidance, the people fall, but in an abundance of counselors, there is safety."

If you're struggling to see a situation clearly, seek the perspective of those who are mature in faith and wisdom. Others can help you slow down and see things from angles you might have missed.

8. Anchor Yourself in God's Promises, Not Your Immediate Feelings.

Feelings fluctuate, but God's character remains constant. Psalm 46:10 urges us,

"Be still, and know that I am God."

When things don't make sense, remind yourself of what is certain—God is good, He is in control, and His purposes will ultimately prevail.

9. *Adopt a Long-Term Perspective on Your Life's Story.*

Imagine looking back on your current situation five years from now. Will you see this moment as a pivotal lesson? A disguised blessing? A necessary detour? Tactical patience means embracing the reality that what feels confusing or painful now may one day make perfect sense in the grand story God is writing.

Pause... Breathe... Reflect.

1. Have you confused unexpected turns with wrong turns?

2. Where is God asking you to trust Him, even when you don't have a map?

3. Can you recall a time when a detour became a divine appointment?

Word of God Speak

Psalm 23:4

"Even though I walk through the valley of the shadow of death, I will fear no evil, for you are with me..."

Chapter 9
I – Impact Others with Encouragement

Correction does much, but encouragement does more. Encouragement after censure is as the sun after a shower." Johann Wolfgang von Goethe[76]

As parents, one of the most crucial roles we play is guiding our kids toward a future worth pursuing—a future not centered on self-indulgence or mere self-actualization but on something much greater: using their God-given talents to serve others. In a world that often tells them to chase personal success, fulfillment, or happiness, it's our job to teach them that true purpose is found in how they contribute to the lives of others. When we help them discover their unique giftings and strengths, we're not just giving them tools for personal achievement; we're equipping them to make an impact on the world around them.

A life lived solely for oneself can end up feeling shallow and empty, no matter how much success one achieves. But when we

---

[76] Wenckstern, Otto. *Goethe's Opinions on the World, Mankind, Literature, Science, and Art.* Forgotten Books, 2019.

instill in our children the idea that their abilities are meant to serve and encourage others, we are setting them on a path toward fulfillment that transcends fleeting personal accomplishments. The goal is not just for them to be happy but to live meaningful lives that bring joy to others, creating a ripple effect of goodness and resilience. By guiding them this way, we help them realize that their future is not just about what they can get but about what they can give—turning success into significance.

When our ministry unraveled and we found ourselves effectively unemployed, well-meaning folks lined up with the classic Christian pick-me-ups trying to encourage us: "*God has great things in store for you!*" or "*Your best days are ahead!*" One pastor friend said something like that, and I jokingly shot back, "*Sounds great—I'm just waiting for God to clue me in!*"

His reply? "*God's waiting on you!*"

Cue the existential spiral. Suddenly, every platitude felt like a puzzle. *Best days ahead?* Did that mean more money? A leadership role I'd always dreamed of? Or, knowing the Kingdom's track record, more suffering disguised as growth? Was "great things" code for success or another round of character-building trials? Honestly, I knew people were just trying to encourage us, but in the moment, their words felt more like riddles than reassurance. Maybe I was just overthinking it—or maybe God's great plan was to keep me guessing. All these precious people meant well, and their words weren't mere flattery. Still, it struck me—truly impacting others with encouragement demands intention and purpose, not just a string of pretty words.

In the murky depths of 7th grade, I found myself in the curious position of being both a budding musician and a fledgling[77] athlete. Yes, kids, hard to believe, but there was a time when your old man was somewhat sporty!

One day, my teacher, a beacon of encouragement in a sea of adolescent uncertainty, summoned me to assist in distributing papers to my peers. As I made my way to the front of the class, my foot snagged on a heater near the wall, sending me tumbling forward. Miraculously, I managed to save myself from a full-on faceplant with a clumsy yet effective extra step. The class erupted in laughter, but just as quickly as the chuckles began, they were silenced by the sage words of my teacher, "Well done for catching yourself! Being athletic definitely has its perks!"

In that moment, he didn't just prevent me from becoming the day's entertainment; he showed me the power of purposeful encouragement in the face of embarrassment. His actions spoke volumes about his values, and to this day, I'm reminded of the

---

[77] **Fledgling**: New, inexperienced, or just beginning.

importance of intentionally and thoughtfully lifting others up when they stumble, both literally and figuratively.

True Encouragement Speaks at the Right Time

Emily P. Freeman, in *The Next Right Thing*, reminds us of a critical truth: as followers of Jesus, we often feel the urge to rush people toward comfort in the face of their pain. She writes, "It can be easy to refuse to let people grieve the way they need to grieve by naming their circumstances for them, saying phrases like, 'God is in control' or 'Consider it all joy!' or 'God works all things together for good.' He is, it is, and He does. But we are all on our own journey of living into those truths."[78] Her wisdom hits hard because it points to a reality we often ignore—our discomfort with others' pain can make us poor listeners and even poorer encouragers. Instead of offering the sacred gift of presence, we tie up their grief in neat theological bows that may be true but not necessarily helpful in the moment. Sometimes, the best thing we can do for a friend in the depths of despair is to sit quietly and simply *be*. This was the one thing Job's friends initially got right. When they first arrived, they sat with him in silence for seven days, sharing in his suffering without offering solutions (Job 2:13). The trouble began the moment they opened their mouths and

---

[78] Freeman, E. P. (2019). *The Next Right Thing: A Simple, Soulful Practice for Making Life Decisions.* Revell.

presumed to speak for God in Job's pain, assigning blame, oversimplifying his suffering, and ultimately misrepresenting God's character. Let us take a cue from their early silence and learn to honor the sacred process of grief by allowing others—and ourselves—the space to name our own narratives, wrestle with the hard truths of life, and walk a little way into God's promises in due time. Sometimes, encouragement looks less like answers and more like silence.

Every so often, life just feels and is brutal. When things are really difficult, hurtful, and exhausting, well-meaning people usually try to lift our spirits—and while they mean well, their words can sometimes miss the mark. When a tree fell on our house, friends and family reached out with encouraging words: "*It'll all work out*," "*The insurance will take care of everything*," or "*Just hang in there; it'll be fine*." Their kindness was real, and their hearts were in the right place. But the reality we faced was much messier. Dealing with the insurance became a drawn-out struggle; at times, we felt like fish out of water, navigating a sea of red tape and feeling helpless against it.

This experience taught me something about encouragement. There's an art to it. Sometimes, to soften the blow, people offer assurances that, though comforting, may not be fully true. These half-promises can paint a reality that doesn't hold up, leaving us feeling even more isolated, disillusioned, and misunderstood when things don't resolve quickly or easily. True encouragement goes deeper than glossing over the pain. It acknowledges the real struggle without diminishing it, showing empathy without sugar-coating the process. Sometimes, the most encouraging thing you can say isn't that "*Everything will be okay*," but rather, "*This is tough, and I'm here for you*." Recognizing the hardship for what it is makes space for both honesty and hope, two essential anchors in truly resilient support.

God's Heart is to Encourage

When my wife was pregnant with our firstborn, Samuel, you'd think she'd be the one falling apart, right? Nope. That was all me. While Marsha gracefully navigated pregnancy, I was having an existential crisis. I felt wildly underprepared to be a dad. I mean, I couldn't even keep a houseplant alive or change the sparkplug on our lawnmower, and now I was supposed to raise a human being? I wrestled with God over the purpose of fatherhood, devoured every parenting book I could find, prayed like my life depended on it (mine and the life of my kids), and interrogated every dad I knew. Still, I felt like I was standing on the edge of a cliff with no parachute.

Then, one day, in my turmoil, I felt the Lord nudging me to Colossians 3:18-21, where Paul lays out the "household code." He starts with the women as wives, which I thought was smart—ladies first. Then he drops a bombshell for husbands: love your wives and don't be harsh with them. Revolutionary for that time! Then Paul addresses the kids—basic stuff, listen to your parents, follow the rules, etc. But here's the kicker: he never circles back to ladies as mothers. Why? Because Paul knew moms had it down. And my wife proved it. Once Samuel was born, she just knew what to do. It was like God downloaded the mothering playbook straight into her soul. Moms are wired with this incredible ability to nurture, and it was humbling to watch.

But Paul wasn't done with the men yet, though. Oh no, he turned that stiff-necked dad spotlight right on us and said,

"Fathers, do not embitter your children, or they will become discouraged."

Boom. There it was—our number one job: to make sure our kids walk through life encouraged, with their heads held high. That was a game-changer for me. Sure, discipline is part of the gig, but at the end of the day, my primary role isn't to be a taskmaster or a perfection enforcer—it's to be my kids' biggest cheerleader.

The reason why Paul could say that with such confidence was because he knew it reflected the very heart of God. Our heavenly Father disciplines us, yes, but His ultimate goal is to build us up, to encourage us, to remind us of our worth, and to reassure us to walk boldly in His love. Learning that didn't just change my perspective on being a dad; it redefined it. Suddenly, I wasn't falling apart anymore—I had a purpose. And as for my kids? Well, they're lucky they got their mom, too. Let's just say God knew what He was doing when He didn't leave parenting up to me alone.

You Can't Pour From an Empty Cup: Learn to be Encouraged First

It is God's heart to build up, encourage, fortify, and strengthen humans, His sons and daughters. In the grand tapestry of creation, humanity stands as a masterpiece woven with intricate threads of divine design, value, and purpose. Resilience is fueled by a desire to fight, to rise up again, and to overcome obstacles. But if we lack a clear, accurate view of ourselves, that strength will be hard to find. We can't be encouraged, and in turn, we won't be able to truly encourage others. Knowing that we're created in the image of God—marked with infinite worth and value—changes everything. When we grasp this truth, we understand that we're not just getting back up because life demands it or because we're stubborn. Instead, we rise because we know that God has given us a purpose, strength, and dignity that is unshakable. Believing in our God-given worth gives us the courage to face challenges head-on, to keep pushing forward, and to develop the resilience that life so often requires.

The most encouraging truth, especially amid chaos, is that you are infinitely valuable, not because of what you do or achieve, but simply because of who made you. You deserve to be celebrated, not just for your successes but for your efforts, your perseverance, and your uniqueness. You deserve to be encouraged, to have someone in your corner cheering you on, believing in you even when you struggle to believe in yourself. You deserve support, a helping hand when you stumble, a shoulder to lean on when you're weary, and a listening ear when you need to share your thoughts and feelings. You deserve to be cheered on, to have someone applaud your victories, no matter how small they may seem to others, and to remind you of your worth, especially when you forget it yourself.

You are not merely a product of chance or evolutionary processes; you are an intentional creation of a loving and purposeful God. Being made in the image of God is fundamentally about status, not attributes. It means that every human being has inherent dignity, worth, and value simply by being human. This status is not based on our abilities, achievements, or appearance but on the fact that we are created in the likeness of God himself. It means that each one of us possesses a sacredness that is irreplaceable and irreducible. This truth radically alters how we view ourselves and others. It calls us to recognize and honor the divine imprint[79] in every human being, treating each person with respect, kindness, and compassion. My teacher in 7th grade modeled that perfectly. He taught me that resilience doesn't mean you're never embarrassed or that people won't laugh. It means that you're willing to stand up, dust off, and keep moving, regardless. His words—and the way he looked past my mishap and saw potential—gave me the courage to face not just the snickers of my classmates but so many other "stumbles" life threw my way. Looking back, I see that his small act of belief was one of the most powerful early lessons in resilience I could have asked for.

Cultivating Self-Worth as the Soil for Resilience

First, you need to let yourself be encouraged before you can be an encourager. But for encouragement to grow, it needs healthy soil—a foundation of self-worth that can hold it steady when the winds blow. Without this core sense of value, encouragement and resilience can feel like an uphill climb, a struggle against doubt and insecurity. Yet, when we embrace the truth of our worth, grounded in God's love, we build a sturdy ground from which resilience can flourish.

It's easy to say, "Believe in your worth," but in practice, this

---

[79] **Divine imprint**: The belief that every human bears the image or likeness of God.

can be challenging. We're often bombarded with messages that subtly chip away at our value. Society may tell us our worth depends on our performance, looks, or status. However, the Bible paints a different picture. Our value is not earned; it's given. God declares in Isaiah 43:4,

"You are precious and honored in my sight, and I love you."

When this truth is our foundation, we become more resilient because we know that no failure, rejection, or storm can take away our inherent worth.

Drawing inspiration from John Maxwell's *The 15 Invaluable Laws of Growth,*[80] here are a few thoughts on how to build self-esteem, cultivate resilience, and in turn become an encourager of others:

1. Guard Your Self-Talk.

When my kids were younger, I tried to teach them that words have incredible power—the power to lift others up or tear them down. It's a simple truth but often a hard lesson to grasp, and it didn't always sink in quickly. They could be sharp with one another, saying things that stung deeply, sometimes without realizing how much those words could actually hurt. I wanted them

---

[80] Maxwell, J. C. (2012). *The 15 Invaluable Laws of Growth: Live Them and Reach Your Potential.* Center Street.

to understand that the words we speak not only impact others but also circle back to shape us. The things we say echo in our own ears, and what we hear repeatedly can settle into our hearts, influencing how we see ourselves and shaping who we ultimately become. Words, once spoken, can build resilience, courage, joy, and hope, or they can sow seeds of insecurity, anger, or resentment. It's a lesson that takes time to learn: our words are not only arrows or lifelines we cast out toward others; they are reflections that return to us, forging our inner lives. I still remind them that choosing words wisely and with kindness is a way of shaping both our relationships and our own hearts.

Self-worth can easily be undermined by the inner critic, a voice that doubts, compares, and condemns. But the Bible encourages us to

"take every thought captive to make it obedient to Christ" (2 Corinthians 10:5).

Acknowledge and challenge negative self-talk by confronting it with the truth of who God says you are.

"For we are God's handiwork, created in Christ Jesus to do good works, which God prepared in advance for us to do."

(Ephesians 2:10).

When negative thoughts arise, pause and write them down.

Counter each thought with a truth from scripture.

The conversations you have with yourself are powerful. They shape your confidence, mindset, and how you navigate challenges. Every day, you're either building yourself up or tearing yourself down with your internal dialogue. Replace self-criticism with affirmations of your worth and potential. For example, instead of saying, *"I'll never get this right,"* shift to, *"I'm learning, and I'll get better with time."* Speak kindly to yourself as you would to a close friend. Over time, this practice will help you face life's challenges with greater confidence and clarity.

2. *Avoid Unhealthy Comparisons.*

Nothing erodes self-esteem faster than comparing yourself to others. It's tempting to scroll through social media or glance at a coworker's success and feel inadequate. But comparisons only focus on external achievements and rarely tell the full story. Instead, focus on your journey and measure progress by how far you've come, not how far others are ahead. Compare yourself to the person you were yesterday and celebrate small wins along the way. This shift will help you embrace your unique path and stay motivated.

Comparison, as highlighted by one of my Clifton Strengths,[81]

---

[81] **Clifton Strengths:** A test that helps people find out what they're naturally good at.

can be a double-edged sword. On the one hand, it can drive us to achieve greater heights by benchmarking our progress against others, fostering a sense of healthy competition and motivation. Recognizing and appreciating the achievements of others can serve as a powerful catalyst for personal growth. However, the darker side of comparison lies in its potential to erode self-worth. When used in an unhealthy manner, comparison can lead to constant self-criticism and a relentless pursuit of perfectionism. This not only undermines our own sense of value but also diminishes our ability to genuinely celebrate and encourage the successes of others. Instead of being a source of inspiration, comparison becomes a tool for self-sabotage, fostering feelings of inadequacy and envy.

By being mindful of how we use this strength, we can ensure it remains a positive force in our lives, driving us to be our best without undermining our self-worth or the support we offer to others.

3. Challenge Limiting Beliefs.

Limiting beliefs are those nagging doubts that whisper, "*You're not good enough*" or "*This will never work.*" These thoughts can be paralyzing if left unchecked. To overcome them, you must first identify them. Ask yourself, "*Is this thought helping or hindering me?*" Replace "*I can't*" with "*What steps can I take?*" or "*How can I grow through this?*"

Remember, growth doesn't require certainty—just the courage to take the next step. When you move away from negative assumptions, you open the door to unexpected possibilities.

4. Add Value To Others.

There's a deep connection between impacting others and improving your self-esteem. When you shift your focus outward and help someone else, whether through encouragement, service, or acts of kindness, you begin to see your own value more clearly. Adding value doesn't have to be monumental; small gestures can make a big difference. This practice not only strengthens your relationships but also builds a sense of purpose and fulfillment in your own life.

5. Engage In What Matters.

Your ability to grow in self-esteem and resilience often comes down to your daily decisions. Trust your instincts to guide you toward what feels meaningful and right. This might mean pursuing a passion project, setting boundaries in toxic relationships, or staying disciplined in your personal and spiritual life. Resilience isn't just about surviving challenges—it's about thriving in alignment with your values. By focusing on what truly matters, you cultivate confidence and create a life rooted in purpose.

Scripture serves as the ultimate mirror, reflecting who we are in God's eyes. Instead of relying on our own feelings, we need to root our identity in His Word. For instance, in Psalm 139:13-14, David marvels at being "fearfully and wonderfully made," celebrating that every part of us is carefully crafted by God. Meditate on verses that speak of your worth and purpose. Write down these scriptures, place them somewhere visible, and read them aloud daily. Let them become an anchor in your heart and mind.

Choose a few scriptures, such as Ephesians 2:10 ("For we are God's handiwork"), Romans 8:38-39 (about God's unshakeable love), and 1 John 3:1 ("See what great love the Father has lavished on us"), and memorize them. When doubt creeps in, repeat these verses, reaffirming that your value is found in God's words, not the world's shifting standards.

When we struggle with self-worth, we often see ourselves through a lens of past mistakes, shortcomings, or the opinions of others. Prayer is a powerful way to ask God to replace this distorted view with His perspective. Remember, Jesus himself said,

"Ask, and it will be given to you" (Matthew 7:7).

Pray for a clear vision of who you are in His eyes, asking Him to reveal your identity and worth.

Set aside 5-10 minutes daily for prayer specifically focused on your self-worth. Ask God to reveal His love and purpose for you. Write down any impressions, feelings, or scriptures that come to mind during this time. Over time, you'll notice a shift as you begin to see yourself more as He sees you.

Self-worth flourishes when we feel connected to our purpose. By engaging in activities that reflect God's calling—whether serving others, creating, or learning something new—we experience a sense of fulfillment and alignment with who God created us to be. 1 Corinthians 12:4-7 reminds us that each of us has unique gifts given by the Spirit "for the common good." Using these gifts validates our worth and brings glory to God.

Make a list of activities that bring you joy, align with your gifts, and serve others. Begin incorporating these into your life consistently, even if it's just a small act of kindness each day or volunteering once a month. These activities reinforce that your life has meaning, value, and purpose.

Self-worth grows in an environment of love and affirmation. Surround yourself with people who see you through God's eyes and encourage you to grow in faith. Proverbs 27:17 says,

"As iron sharpens iron, so one person sharpens another."

Being in a community helps us see our value reflected in

others' love and encouragement, building a support system that upholds us during tough times.

Seek out a church group, Bible study, or a few close friends who are rooted in faith. Make it a priority to spend time with them regularly, engaging in open, honest conversations. This network of faith-driven people will offer support and wisdom, reminding you of your value when doubts arise.

When self-worth is grounded in God's truth, you don't have to fight for your own significance and are enabled to encourage others in their journey. Resilience becomes a natural response to life's challenges. Rooted in the knowledge of our value as His children, we can withstand trials and setbacks without crumbling under the weight of doubt and insecurity. By immersing ourselves in scripture, challenging negative self-talk, praying for God's perspective, engaging in purposeful activities, and surrounding ourselves with a supportive community, we cultivate a life resilient not in our own strength but in the unwavering truth of our identity in Christ. First, encourage yourself in the Lord and then truly encourage others.

One final thought on growing in self-worth so that we can effectively encourage others: we've explored principles and practices to help us root our identity in Jesus, stand firm in who we are, and cultivate strength. But if our pursuit of self-worth ever overshadows the pursuit of God's worth, we have lost our way.

True self-worth is not found in self-exploration alone—it is discovered in the overwhelming beauty and majesty of Jesus. When we fix our eyes on Him in worship, we stop striving to *prove* our value, and instead, we *receive* it. The more we gaze upon His splendor, the more we see ourselves rightly—not as the center of the universe, but as deeply loved, chosen, and secure in Him.

Ultimately, self-worth is not about self-promotion; it is about His fame in the world. It is not about our own comfort but about His kingdom coming and His will being done. If our journey toward self-assurance makes us more self-absorbed instead of more Christ-absorbed, we are building on sand. But when we seek *His* righteousness first—when we pursue *His* beauty, *His* kingdom, *His* glory—we will find, often unexpectedly, that our own worth is settled, unshakable, and anchored in something far greater than ourselves.

Jesus never called us to find ourselves apart from Him—He called us to lose ourselves in Him. And in that glorious surrender, we are found and are powerfully equipped to encourage others.

Encouragement Versus Flattery

Dale Carnegie's *How to Win Friends and Influence People*[82] is

---

[82] Carnegie, D. (2020). *How To Win Friends And Influence People*. Sristhi

208

a timeless guide to improving interpersonal skills and building positive relationships. Published back in 1936, the book offers practical advice on how to connect with others, influence their behavior, and foster meaningful connections. Carnegie's principles are based on the idea that genuine interest and respect for others are key to successful interactions.

Carnegie makes a clear distinction between true encouragement and flattery. He emphasizes that genuine appreciation and encouragement are rooted in sincerity and respect, while flattery is shallow and self-serving. Effective encouragement is specific and detailed. Instead of making vague compliments, focus on particular achievements or traits. Genuine encouragement involves understanding and empathizing with the other person's feelings and experiences. Genuine encouragement aims to inspire and motivate the other person to continue their positive behavior or efforts.

Flattery is often insincere and motivated by self-interest. It lacks genuine appreciation and respect. It tends to be vague and general, lacking specific details or examples. Flattery is often used as a tool for manipulation, aiming to gain favor or advantage. It may provide a temporary boost, but it lacks the lasting impact of

---

Publishers & Distributors.

true encouragement.

Carnegie argues that true encouragement, rooted in sincerity and genuine appreciation, is far more effective in building positive relationships and influencing others. Flattery, on the other hand, is easily recognized as shallow and self-serving, and it ultimately fails to create meaningful connections. So, we got to receive encouragement and then choose to be a voice of encouragement to the world around us.

Pause... Breathe... Reflect.

1. When was the last time your words gave someone life?
2. Are you withholding encouragement because you think it's too small to matter?
3. Who has God placed in your life right now who needs your voice of hope?

Word of God Speak

Hebrews 10:24–25

"Let us consider how we may spur one another on toward love and good deeds..."

Chapter 10
V – Value God's Word

I'm writing this with a green weather-worn Bible open beside me. My dad placed it in my hands back in 1991. I was ten, too young to truly appreciate the weight of the pages, but old enough to feel the weight of his words penned on the first leaf: "Son, don't ever forget… Jesus is always with you."

My dad never stopped reminding us of that truth. When I was a restless teenager, he'd sometimes gather the family after dinner, open Scripture, and read aloud. I can still picture Christmas Eve: tree lights flickering, presents waiting, my eyes fixed on shiny boxes while his voice drifted through Luke's nativity. At the time, I thought those moments were interruptions. Now, I know they were foundations. I'm so grateful for my dad.

The Bible became my companion through late-night doubts, heartbreaks, and the long stretch of adult questions. Its pages and margins are crowded with underlines and raw prayers. It's an honest record of God meeting me again and again. Over the years, I've learned that this book isn't a self-help manual designed to give me a smoother ride. It's first and foremost a revelation of this astonishing God, Father, Son, Spirit, who invites ordinary, restless people into His story. Yes, there's solid historical, literary, scholarly, and manuscript evidence that anchors the Bible's credibility, but that's not why I keep returning to its pages. I return because they unveil Jesus…the One who bled and died for humanity, walks with us, and calls us to become like Him. And becoming like Him, as M. Robert Mulholland reminds us, is "a dynamic and ever-developing growth toward wholeness in the image of Christ."[83] That unpredictable journey is impossible without the fresh breath of the Word of God.

"All Scripture is breathed out by God and profitable for teaching, for reproof, for correction, and for training in righteousness, that the man of God may be complete, equipped for every good work."
(2 Timothy 3:16-17)

Sometimes the Bible feels messy—genealogies,[84] lament, brutal wars—much like life itself. Yet in wrestling with its mess, my own resilience has deepened. I'm eternally thankful for those teenage and young adult years spent poring over Scripture; all the late-night youth studies, honest questions in small groups, and countless church gatherings. Those were invaluable hours that anchored God's Word in my heart and soul and set the trajectory

---

[83] Mulholland, M. R., Jr. (n.d.). *Invitation to a Journey: A Road Map for Spiritual Formation.* InterVarsity Press.)
[84] **Genealogy:** A record of a line of descent traced continuously from an ancestor.

for my life. When ministry unraveled, when the oak crashed through our roof, when guilt and doubt fogged our vision, His Word steadied us and whispered, "Keep going; the Author is still active." So this chapter isn't a lecture on why you should read the Bible; it's an invitation to meet the God who has met me countless times in these pages.

In the grand tapestry of human history, no other book has sparked as much debate, inspired as much devotion, generated as many resilient hearts, or endured as much scrutiny as the Bible. For millennia, its words have guided the faithful, comforted the afflicted, changed nations, and challenged the complacent.[85] Its truth transcends time, its wisdom surpasses human understanding, and its message continues to resonate with power and authority, drawing people from every nation, tribe, and tongue into a life-changing encounter with the living God.

It is God's Word to us, and to grow resilient, it has to be central to our lives. We ought to make it a daily habit to dive into the Bible. Remember, we're not worshipping a book here; we're uncovering the very heart of the One we worship.

Sure, there are parts that might seem like a tangled mess. That's because the Bible isn't a tidy manual; it's a sprawling epic, a

---

[85] **Complacent**: Self-satisfied and unaware of possible dangers or deficiencies.

grand narrative of God's relentless pursuit of His people amidst the chaos we've woven. God rarely just hands out answers; He unfolds stories. In our need for control, we often demand answers—why things happen, when relief will come, or how a crisis will resolve.

Yet, God doesn't always answer us directly, nor does He always reveal His purposes in full. Instead, He invites us to trust Him in the unfolding of a greater story. Scripture shows us time and again that God works through seasons of uncertainty, not by providing instant clarity but by calling His people to walk by faith. Abraham didn't know where he was going, but he trusted the God who promised to lead him. Joseph couldn't see how betrayal and imprisonment would lead to redemption, yet somehow, he remained faithful, knowing that God was writing a story far bigger than his immediate suffering.

When we demand every answer upfront, we miss the beauty of the journey. God's narrative is often one of slow revelation, of building trust in the unknown, of moving forward without seeing the whole picture. This is where resilience is born—not in certainty, but in the willingness to keep going, to endure, and to grow in the midst of unanswered questions. We don't need all the answers to be resilient. What we need is trust in God's faithfulness and a willingness to lean into His grace as our story unfolds. He is inviting us to walk with Him through the mystery, the process, and the unfolding grace.

We can approach the Scriptures with a sense of wonder and curiosity, especially when we stumble upon passages that leave us scratching our heads. Life isn't always neat and orderly, and neither is the Bible. Embrace the mysteries and uncertainties. And remember, the goal isn't to have it all figured out but to draw closer to the God whose victorious story is being unveiled before you.

How to Immerse Yourself in the Bible as the Generous Self-Revelation of God

Start with prayer. Prayer is essential before reading the Bible because it opens our hearts and minds to receive God's wisdom and understanding. When we pray, we acknowledge our dependence on God's Spirit to illuminate the Scriptures for us. After all, He is the author of it. This practice humbles us, recognizing that without the guidance of the Holy Spirit, our interpretations for sure we'll be flawed. Through prayer, we invite God to speak to us through His Word, aligning our hearts with His voice and will.

Consistency in reading the Bible is also key to spiritual growth and becoming familiar with its tone and linguistics. Just as we need regular nourishment for our bodies, our spirit needs regular feeding from God's Word. Setting aside a specific time each day helps establish a routine that can become a cherished habit. This regularity allows us to delve deeper into the Word, uncovering its richness and applying its truths to our lives. A good reading plan can provide structure and direction to our Bible reading. It ensures that we cover a variety of passages, including those that may be challenging or unfamiliar. Reading plans can also help us see the overarching narrative of the Bible, from creation to redemption, highlighting God's love and faithfulness throughout history. Without a grasp of the greater narrative, specifics plotline won't really make sense.

The Bible is an epic story, spanning from the creation of the universe to the promise of a new heaven and earth. It's like a vast tapestry intricately woven with stories of love, betrayal, redemption, and hope. In Genesis, we witness the dawn of creation, with God sculpting the world and all its wonders. From the breathtaking beauty of the Garden of Eden to the tragic fall of humanity through Adam and Eve's egocentric disobedience, Genesis sets the stage for the overarching narrative of God's pursuit of His people.

As we journey through the Old Testament, we encounter the patriarchs and matriarchs—Abraham, Sarah, Isaac, Rebekah, Jacob, and Joseph—whose stories are woven into the fabric of God's purposes. We witness the miraculous exodus of the Israelites from slavery in Egypt, led by Moses and guided by the mighty hand of God. The parting of the Red Sea, the giving of the Ten Commandments, and the wandering in the wilderness all serve as reminders of God's faithfulness and provision. The historical books of the Old Testament—Joshua, Judges, Samuel, and Kings—paint a vivid picture of Israel's tumultuous history, filled with triumphs and tragedies. We see the rise and fall of kings, the prophetic voices of Elijah and Elisha, and the exile and return of God's people. The wisdom literature of the Old Testament—Job, Psalms, Proverbs, Ecclesiastes, and Song of Solomon—offers timeless insights into the human experience, exploring themes of suffering, joy, wisdom, and love. The Psalms, in particular, express the full range of human emotions, from lament and despair to praise and thanksgiving.

In the New Testament, we encounter the life, death, and resurrection of Jesus Christ—the ultimate expression of God's love for humanity. Jesus' teachings, miracles, and sacrificial death on the cross reveal God's unending grace and His purpose for salvation and redemption. The early church, as recorded in the book of Acts, is a testament to the transformative power of the gospel and the work of the Holy Spirit. The epistles,[86] or letters, written by the apostles offer practical guidance for Christian living and theology. Paul's letters, in particular, address issues of faith,

---

[86] **Epistles**: Letters in the New Testament written by apostles to early Christian communities.

grace, and the importance of unity in the body of Christ. However, remember that these letters were written to certain people at a particular time in a specific cultural context. Lastly, the book of Revelation highlights the final victory of God over evil and the establishment of a new heaven and earth, where God's kingdom will reign forever.

The Bible is not just a collection of random stories; it is the story of God's love and faithfulness to His people. It is a story of redemption, salvation, hope, and the promise of a future restored. Everything that is out of order will come back into order. Again, without a grasp of the greater narrative of scripture, specifics plotline won't really make sense. Reading passages in context is crucial for understanding their intended meaning. Context includes the verses surrounding a passage, the chapter, the book, and even the entire Bible. Context helps us avoid misinterpretation and allows us to grasp the author's original intent. For example, reading Jesus' parables in the context of His audience and cultural background gives us deeper insight into His teachings.

There are many study tools, such as concordances, dictionaries, and commentaries, that can enhance our understanding of the Bible. They provide historical and cultural background, explain difficult words or concepts, and offer different perspectives on interpretation. However, it's important to use these tools wisely, recognizing that they are secondary to the Bible itself and should not replace personal reflection and prayer.

As we read, we should reflect on how the Scriptures apply to our daily lives. This application may involve changes in our attitudes, behaviors, or relationships. Applying Scripture helps us grow in faith and live according to God's will. While it's important to gain knowledge of the Bible, true understanding goes beyond mere facts. It involves grasping the deeper meaning of Scripture and how it applies to our lives. Understanding requires reflection, prayer, conversation, and a willingness to let God's Word transform us from the inside out.

Discussing the Bible with others can provide new insights and perspectives. It allows us to learn from others' experiences and interpretations, enriching our own understanding. Group discussions, Bible studies, or simply talking with a friend can deepen our appreciation for God's Word and its relevance to our lives. Humility, teachability, and curiosity are essential when reading the Bible because our understanding is limited. We should approach Scripture with an open heart and mind, willing to be corrected and challenged. God's Word is living and active, and it has the power to transform us if we approach it with humility and openness.

Bible study doesn't have to be dull. You can study the Bible verse by verse. You can do a topical study or study a particular character within the story of scripture. You can study an entire book of the Bible, analyzing its structure, themes, authorship, and historical context. You can do a comparative or a historical-cultural study. You can use a journal as you read and spend time in devotion over what you're reading. The Bible doesn't just enrich your life but has the ability to lead your life if you let it. Don't just read the Bible to confirm existing beliefs, which can lead to a skewed understanding of Scripture. It's important to read the entire Bible to grasp its full message and overall narrative and always be open to the molding of our hearts and minds by the Holy Spirit. While personal reflection is invaluable, it's important to consider the interpretations of biblical scholars and theologians. Their insights can provide a deeper understanding of Scripture and help us avoid misinterpretation. Above all, reading the Bible without seeking the guidance of the Holy Spirit can lead to misapprehension. Before diving into the Word, remember, it's like trying to learn to swim without water if we don't pray for God's wisdom and presence first.

The Greatest Story

The way we experience reality is always based on a story. What story shapes our reality? Is there a narrative more significant than others? I dare say the story of God reigns supreme. God's story, His words, His commandments, and His presence are the best description of reality. If we choose to ignore or even intentionally replace them as our foundation for life, we will sooner or later attempt to build our own Tower of Babel.

The issue with the Tower of Babel was that humanity sought to make a name for themselves and reach heaven on their own terms, defying God's design for unity through dependence on Him..

God's story, woven throughout history and revealed in His Word, is a story of true forgiveness, transformation, and freedom.

In the grand tapestry of human existence, the story of Jesus stands as the pinnacle of redemption and hope.

Born into humble beginnings, He walked among the broken and the lost, offering healing to the sick, comfort to the weary, forgiveness to sinners, and hope to the hopeless. His life reflected the power of love and kindness, as He showed compassion to the outcast and mercy to the sinner. But it was His ultimate sacrifice on the cross that truly revealed His Father's heart. In a selfless act of atonement, Jesus bore the weight of humanity's sins upon His shoulders, enduring unimaginable pain and suffering. Yet even amid agony, His words were a declaration of victory, for through His death, sin was defeated, and redemption was made possible. The power of His forgiveness and atonement reverberates through the ages, offering salvation to all who believe. As the sun set on that fateful day, the world was forever changed, and the promise of eternal life was sealed in the blood of the Lamb.

The story of Jesus does not end at the cross, for on the third day, He rose triumphantly from the grave, conquering death itself. His resurrection was not only a demonstration of His divine power but also a fulfillment of prophecy and a vindication of His identity as the Son of God. The resurrection is central to the Christian faith, as it signifies the victory of light over darkness, life over death, and hope over despair. Through His resurrection, Jesus offers us the promise of new life, both now and for eternity. His victory over death is a reminder that no matter how deep our sins or how insurmountable our struggles, there is always hope in Christ. The resurrection is not just an event in history but a reality that continues to transform lives today, reminding us that the story of God is one of redemption, restoration, and unending love.

When we align our lives with God's narrative, His commandments and words become a roadmap, strengthening our hearts and guiding us through the complexities of life with resilience. They not only inform our values but also mold our character.

At the end of the day, our love for God's Word is not just about knowledge—it's about transformation. Scripture is not a book we merely study; it is a voice we heed, a light we follow, and a foundation we stand on when everything else crumbles. So, don't just have a Bible on your nightstand, but carry His words in your hearts. His Word is alive, and it does not return void (Isaiah 55:11). It corrects, strengthens, guides, and sustains. If we treat it lightly, we rob ourselves of the very wisdom, power, and life God has given to us. But if we treasure and value it—if we plant it deep in our hearts and let it define our steps—then we will be like a tree firmly planted by streams of water, bearing fruit in every season (Psalm 1:2-3). In a world full of shifting opinions and fleeting truths, let us be people who are unshakable, resilient, standing firm on the one foundation that will never fail: the living and eternal Word of God.

Pause... Breathe... Reflect.

1. Is God's Word your first stop for direction—or your last resort?

2. How would your day change if you truly believed His Word was alive and active?

3. What promise from Scripture do you need to cling to in this season?

Word of God Speak

Psalm 119:105

"Your word is a lamp to my feet and a light to my path."

Chapter 11
E – Evaluate With Grace

Recovering from trauma and building resilience is a journey that requires a lot of grace. It's a deeply emotional, spiritual, and practical process. Trauma leaves its fingerprints on the amygdala, the part of the brain that governs our fight, flight, or freeze responses. After a traumatic experience, this part of our brain often becomes hypersensitive, reacting not only to actual threats but also to reminders, echoes, or even harmless cues that feel connected to the original pain. The challenge is retraining our minds and hearts to not relive those moments over and over again, to stop the cycle of fear and helplessness that trauma imprints on us. And that requires intention, patience, a willingness to face the pain, and a lot of grace with oneself and others.

I saw this starkly in my daughter, Julia. One day, a neighbor's dog tore into our backyard, completely unprovoked, and snatched her beloved guinea pig. The tiny creature didn't stand a chance. Julia witnessed it all. She screamed, cried, and ran to my arms, trembling, asking me over and over again, "Why did this happen?"

In the weeks and months that followed, her entire view of dogs shifted. A creature she once loved now became a source of anxiety and distrust. She'd stiffen and hide behind me if a dog walked by, her little heart racing as though it might break. It was heartbreaking to see, and yet, I knew this was part of the trauma working its way into her mind. We couldn't just tell her to "get over it." Healing wouldn't come through dismissal or avoidance. It came through sitting with her in her fear, listening to her feelings, gently exposing her to dogs again over time, and praying together that God would heal her heart. Slowly, she began to see dogs differently—not as immediate threats, but as creatures that, like life itself, are unpredictable yet redeemable.

The trauma of the tree that hit our house was no different. My wife and daughter were home when it fell, and they heard the earth-shaking crash as the giant oak destroyed everything in its path. It was terrifying and life-altering. For weeks that followed, every rumble of thunder brought fear to the surface. My wife would tense up, her mind racing back to that awful moment, and my daughter would ask, "What if another tree falls?" The trauma lingered, and it wasn't something we could just will away.

When life knocks us down, it's natural to want to get up quickly and push past the pain. But the truth is, rushing through the process of grief, frustration, or sorrow only stifles the growth that can come from it. When we're down, it's essential to stay there for a moment or even for a while—to grieve, to cry, and to fully acknowledge the weight of life's injustices. There's a deep necessity in allowing ourselves to feel the doubt, the pain, the heaviness, and the confusion that often accompany life's hardest moments.

Crying out to God, even in anger or frustration, doesn't show weakness or lack of faith; rather, it shows that we're engaging with the reality of our pain. The Bible is full of people like David, Job, and Jeremiah who wrestled openly with God through their trials (Psalm 22:1, Job 3:11, Lamentations 3). If we don't allow ourselves to evaluate with grace and instead rush to move on, we not only miss the profound lessons embedded in our suffering, but we also don't allow our hearts to "unload" and heal.

True resilience is not born from simply getting up, but from staying down long enough to evaluate with grace, process the hurt, face the fear, and slowly rise again, stronger, wiser, and more grounded. It's in those vulnerable moments—when the tears flow and the questions are raw—that we are shaped into people who can truly endure and thrive through adversity. Allowing yourself to grieve fully creates the foundation for a resilience that isn't shallow but deeply anchored in the realities of life and faith. So, scream if you must, yell at God (not so much at people), feel, cry, ask, walk, lie, sleep.

In times of chaos and adversity, evaluating with grace can be a beacon of hope and stability. Often, we're quick to jump to conclusions and seek immediate solutions, but taking a moment to reflect and approach the situation with grace allows for deeper understanding and compassion. Grace, a divine gift from God in salvation, is not just a spiritual concept but a practical tool we can choose to embody in our daily lives. It enables us to evaluate ourselves, others, and the circumstances we face with a kind and forgiving heart. By walking in grace, we extend patience and empathy, fostering an environment where healing and growth can flourish amidst turmoil. This intentional choice to embrace grace in challenging times transforms our interactions and perceptions, creating a ripple effect of positivity and resilience.

Graceful Self-Evaluation

Evaluating oneself with grace is a powerful practice that fosters growth and self-awareness. Start with mindful reflection,[87] setting aside dedicated time to calmly think about your actions, your surroundings, your trauma, thoughts, and feelings. Again, journaling can be a great tool for this, allowing you to express yourself freely and explore your inner world. Remember to incorporate positive affirmations, reminding yourself of God's presence.

---

[87] **Mindful reflection**: Deliberate, thoughtful contemplation or examination of one's thoughts or actions.

Seeking feedback from trusted friends, family members, or mentors can provide valuable insights and help you see yourself more clearly. Embrace their constructive feedback with an open heart and mind. Practice self-compassion by treating yourself with the same kindness and understanding you would offer a friend. Acknowledge that everyone makes mistakes and focus on how you can improve moving forward.

Setting realistic goals is key to staying motivated without feeling overwhelmed. Break your goals into smaller steps and celebrate your progress along the way. Cultivate a gratitude practice by regularly acknowledging the positive aspects of your life, which can shift your focus from what's lacking to what's abundant. Adopting a growth mindset encourages you to view challenges and setbacks as opportunities for learning and development.

Balance self-criticism with praise by recognizing both your areas for improvement and your successes. Pay attention to your physical well-being as it impacts your mental and emotional state. Engage in activities that promote relaxation and self-care, such as exercise, meditation, and adequate sleep.

Evaluating yourself with grace requires patience and practice, but it can lead to a deeper understanding of yourself and a more compassionate approach to personal growth. Embrace the journey with an open heart, and remember that grace is a gift you can offer yourself and others.

Gracefully Evaluating Tough Situations

Learning to gracefully evaluate tough situations involves cultivating a mindset of patience, empathy, and objectivity. Here are some tips to help you approach difficult situations with grace:

1. ***Pause and Reflect.***

Before reacting, take a moment to pause and collect your thoughts. This brief pause can help you respond more thoughtfully and avoid impulsive reactions.

2. ***Seek Multiple Perspectives.***

Consider different viewpoints to gain a more comprehensive understanding of the situation. This can help you see the bigger picture and avoid biases.

3. ***Practice Empathy.***

Try to put yourself in others' shoes and understand their emotions and motivations. Empathy can help you respond with compassion and fairness.

4. ***Stay Calm and Composed.***

Maintaining your composure can prevent the situation from escalating. Deep breathing, mindfulness, and grounding techniques can help you stay centered.

5. *Ask Open-Ended Questions.*

Instead of making assumptions, ask open-ended questions to gather more information. This can lead to better insights and more constructive conversations.

6. *Focus on Solutions.*

Shift your attention from dwelling on the problem to finding solutions. A positive and proactive approach can lead to more effective outcomes.

7. *Avoid Blame.*

Instead of pointing fingers, focus on understanding the root cause of the issue. A blame-free approach encourages collaboration and problem-solving.

8. *Embrace Flexibility.*

Be open to adjusting your perspective and approach as new information emerges. Flexibility allows you to adapt to changing circumstances gracefully.

9. *Practice Self-Compassion.*

Be kind to yourself and acknowledge that it's okay to make mistakes. Self-compassion helps you maintain a balanced perspective and recover from setbacks.

10. *Cultivate Gratitude.*

Focus on the positive aspects of the situation, even in challenging times. Gratitude can shift your mindset and help you approach difficulties with a more positive outlook.

By integrating these techniques into your daily life, you can develop the ability to evaluate tough situations with grace and compassion. This not only enhances your problem-solving skills but also fosters healthier and more positive interactions with others.

The Beauty and Power of God's Grace in Times of Trouble

The grace of God, an unfathomable and boundless gift, whispers to our souls with a tender and eternal embrace. As we ponder the depths of His grace, epitomized in Ephesians 2:8—*"For by grace you have been saved through faith. And this is not your own doing; it is the gift of God"*—we begin to perceive the transformative power of God's grace in our lives. This divine grace, bestowed upon us unconditionally, beckons us to extend the same compassion towards ourselves and others. It is a gentle reminder that our worth is not defined by our failures or successes but by His unwavering love.

In moments of chaos and adversity, when life's turbulent waves threaten to engulf us, embracing God's grace allows us to evaluate our circumstances with gentleness and understanding. Reflecting on our traumas through the lens of grace cultivates a heart that forgives, heals, and nurtures. As we navigate the complexities of life, grace becomes the balm that soothes our wounds and the light that guides our path. With an understanding of His grace, we learn to forgive ourselves for our shortcomings and extend that same forgiveness to others.

The Apostle Paul's words in Romans 8:38-39 remind us that nothing can separate us from the love of God—neither death nor life, angels nor rulers, things present nor things to come. This profound truth anchors us in the midst of life's storms, reassuring us that we are never alone. Grace, as described in Titus 2:11, brings salvation and teaches us to live upright and godly lives, even in the face of trials. It empowers us to rise above our circumstances, not through our strength but through His.

By internalizing this divine grace, we cultivate a spirit of empathy and compassion. We become more patient, understanding that everyone is fighting their own battles. We learn to see beyond the surface, to the heart of those around us, and offer support rather than judgment. Grace transforms our interactions, making them more meaningful and filled with love. It is a choice we make daily, to walk in grace, and in doing so, we reflect the very nature of God.

Moreover, grace helps us to reframe our perspective on adversity. Instead of seeing challenges as insurmountable obstacles, we view them as opportunities for growth and transformation. As stated in 2 Corinthians 12:9, *His grace is sufficient for us, and His power is made perfect in weakness.* This divine assurance allows us to approach life's difficulties with a sense of peace and resilience, knowing that His strength will carry us through.

In essence, the grace of God is a transformative force that changes how we see ourselves, others, and the world around us. It invites us to embrace our humanity, with all its flaws and imperfections, and find beauty amid brokenness. By walking in and evaluating with grace, we create a ripple effect, spreading love, compassion, and hope to those around us. It is a testament to the power of God's love and a reminder that, even in the darkest times, His grace is sufficient.

Pause... Breathe... Reflect.

1. Are you offering yourself the same grace you extend to others?
2. What areas of your life need truth spoken in love, not shame?
3. Can you see progress in your life even if perfection still feels far off?

Word of God Speak

2 Corinthians 12:9

"But He said to me, 'My grace is sufficient for you, for my power is made perfect in weakness.'"

Epilogue
Muscles and Miracles

Suffering naturally prompts us to question its meaning and purpose, like my daughter Julia did when the dog killed her guinea pig or when the tree hit our house. As believers, when facing hardship, we often wonder: Should we pray for a miracle or focus on enduring with faith? What should our focus be? The fact is, resilience is like a muscle; the more you exercise it, the stronger it becomes.

Children go through various developmental stages, each stage requiring enormous focus, starting from when they're just lying there like tiny, helpless bean sprouts. Then comes the slow, dramatic turn from their back to their stomach, a move that requires Herculean[88] effort in their miniature world. Next up, the grand spectacle of pushing up and mastering the art of crawling, a feat that often involves comical wobbling and frequent tumbles. Parents quickly learn to childproof their homes as their little explorers discover the heights of tables and countertops, usually with their heads.

---

[88] **Herculean**: Requiring great strength or effort.

But the 'fun' doesn't end here. After conquering crawling, kids embark on the shaky journey of sitting up and tentatively attempting to stand. This phase is like watching a wobbly-legged foal trying to find its balance, complete with plenty of falls and bumps along the way. It's during this stage that parents start questioning their interior decorating choices, taking down all the knick-knacks before their toddler can get to them, and padding every corner in the house.

Then, the momentous milestone arrives: walking. Those once-wobbly legs have now strengthened, propelling kids into the exhilarating world of bipedal propulsion.[89] And let's not forget the ultimate achievement—running, a skill that brings sheer joy to kids and mild, if not severe, panic to their parents.

I vividly remember watching my kids go through these stages. One particular memory stands out: the day my son Samuel was determined to turn from his back to his stomach. I was poised to lend a helping hand, but then I felt a nudge from God, as if He were saying to me, "Don't do it. Let him do it himself." Initially puzzled and a tad offended, I held back. To my amazement, Samuel managed to roll over all by himself in just a few minutes. It was a profound lesson in God's ways. Sometimes, when we ask for

---

[89] **Bipedal propulsion**: Movement using two legs; walking or running.

a miracle, God wants to give us a muscle.

When we pray for a miracle that would alleviate or end our pain, we might unknowingly close ourselves off from the deeper work God is seeking to accomplish in us through that very suffering. The trials we often wish away may be the precise moments God uses to shape and refine us, transmuting[90] our brokenness into glory and increasing divine love within us. While God may not be the author of our pain, He uses it in His wisdom to draw us closer to Him and to wean us from the vain ambitions and selfish inclinations that otherwise lead us astray.

Philippians 1:29 reminds us,

"For it has been granted to you on behalf of Christ not only to believe in Him but also to suffer for Him."

Suffering is not an accidental burden but a privilege that draws us into a profound, intimate relationship with Christ, who Himself suffered for us. In this light and focus, resilience takes on a new meaning. It's not merely about bearing up under pressure but learning to let suffering draw us closer to God, trusting that He is using it to prepare us for a purpose we cannot yet see.

The apostle Peter speaks directly to this in 1 Peter 4:12-14:

---

[90] **Transmuting**: Changing in form, nature, or substance.

"Dear friends, do not be surprised at the fiery ordeal that has come on you to test you, as though something strange were happening to you. But rejoice inasmuch as you participate in the sufferings of Christ, so that you may be overjoyed when His glory is revealed."

Peter is calling believers to change their focus and to rejoice in their sufferings, not because suffering itself is necessarily desirable, but because it holds a transformative power. Our natural response to hardship is often to pray for a miracle, a quick resolution that brings relief. Yet, in doing so, we may overlook the possibility that God is more interested in building a spiritual muscle within us. This resilience goes beyond mere survival. Such resilience is woven with divine strength and prepared to endure not only the challenges of this life but also to contribute to God's eternal purposes.

In 1 Peter 5:10, Peter reminds us of God's end goal for our suffering:

"And the God of all grace, who called you to His eternal glory in Christ, after you have suffered a little while, will Himself restore you and make you strong, firm, and steadfast."

Peter points out that suffering is temporary, and it serves a redemptive purpose. The promise of restoration, strength, and steadfastness is part of a process that prepares us both for the challenges of today and for an eternal life with God. Our resilience is not simply the capacity to 'bounce back.' It is the enduring power to trust that every trial we face is under God's sovereign care and will ultimately yield a harvest of righteousness and peace. It's through this kind of resilience that we can *"rejoice in our sufferings,"* as Paul writes in Romans 5:3-5, because we know that suffering produces perseverance, character, and, ultimately, hope.

Therefore, when we pray for miracles, we should do so with open hearts, willing to accept that sometimes God's miracle comes not through instant relief but through His refining work in us. God may indeed answer with deliverance, but there are times when He chooses to answer by fortifying us, building in us a resilient spirit that bears His imprint. In those moments, what we once saw as needless suffering may, in retrospect, reveal itself as God's tool for our earthly and eternal preparation. The hardships we face become more than obstacles to overcome; they become the very means by which we grow in divine love, eternal perspective, renewed focus, and Christ-like character. Resilience, then, is not about merely enduring suffering but allowing God to use it as an instrument of transformation, rooting us deeply in His love and preparing us for His most glorious ends.

Our focus should always be on trusting that God is at work, whether through miraculous intervention or the quieter,

241

transformative power of enduring faith. Whether God delivers us from hardship or strengthens us within it, our calling is to trust, seek His purpose, and allow Him to work in us, making us resilient and steadfast.

Conclusion

Resilience often blooms in the soil of pain, where tears water seeds we never knew were planted. Beauty is not born from perfection but rises defiantly from the ashes, embodying the power of redemption. Revelation doesn't come to the self-assured but is gifted in moments of surrender, when we let go of our need to control and allow grace to meet us in the depths. Truth is not a sterile theory, but it is forged in the fires of life, lived out in the mess, the chaos, and the unrelenting stream of questions. It is given to the humble and the teachable.

So, when you cry, let the tears fall—they are never wasted. When your heart is heavy with questions, do not stop asking; the very act of seeking shapes your faith. And when you behold, fix your eyes on Jesus, the author and perfecter of the story. It's hard to see the light when darkness seems to veil His face, when purpose is buried beneath confusion, but take heart: the sun will rise again. His mercies, tender and steadfast, will meet you in that new morning. Keep walking, keep trusting, keep growing resilient, pray for miracles, grow your muscles, for even in the shadows, love, beauty, and truth are at work, preparing the dawn.